MW00417274

English
Conversation
Practice

English
Conversation
Practice

Grant Taylor

Consulting Editor, McGraw-Hill Book Company; Formerly: Associate Professor of English, Director of American Language Institute, New York University; Senior English Language Advisor, English Language Education Council, Tokyo; English Language Consultant, U.S.I.A.; Chairman, English Language Section, National Association for Foreign Student Affairs; Lecturer in English, Columbia University; Associate Editor, *Thorndike-Barnhart Comprehensive Desk Dictionary*

Tata McGraw Hill Education Private Limited
NEW DELHI

McGraw-Hill Offices

New Delhi New York St Louis San Francisco Auckland Bogotá Caracas Kuala Lumpur Lisbon London Madrid Mexico City Milan Montreal San Juan Santiago Singapore Sydney Tokyo Toronto

Tata McGraw-Hill

ENGLISH CONVERSATION PRACTICE

Copyright © 1967 by The McGraw-Hill Companies, Inc. New York. All rights reserved.
No part of this publication may be reproduced or distributed in any form or by any
means, or stored in a database or retrieval system, without the prior written permission
of the publisher

Tata McGraw-Hill Edition 1975

66th reprint 2010
RYDACRAZRLAYY

Reprinted in India by arrangement with The McGraw-Hill Companies, Inc.,
New York

This edition can be exported from India only by the publishers,
Tata McGraw Hill Education Private Limited

ISBN-13: 978-0-07-099603-8
ISBN-10: 0-07-099603-2

Published by Tata McGraw Hill Education Private Limited,
7 West Patel Nagar, New Delhi 110 008, and printed at
Pushp Print Services, Delhi 110 053

The *McGraw·Hill* Companies

Preface

English Conversation Practice is a textbook intended to be useful for oral practice in English either in the classroom or in the language laboratory. The text is planned for use with adult students who have completed at least a beginning course in English.

In this text, oral class or laboratory work is initiated through four-line conversations, and further practice, in exercise form, is derived from or allied with the conversations. The text is divided into two main parts: the conversations in Part 1 are based on common daily situations such as shopping for groceries, asking the time, expressing thanks, etc.; those in Part 2 emphasize particular structural or lexical features of the language such as irregular verbs, tag questions, final prepositions, noun clauses, etc.

The exercises for the situational conversations in Part 1 are based on key sentences from the conversations. At the beginning of each exercise, the line (or lines) in the conversations from which the key sentence was taken is noted. For pedagogical purposes, in a few instances the key sentence for an exercise has been changed to a slightly different form from that of the sentence referred to in a particular conversation. The structure and word study exercises in Part 2 are based on the structural or lexical feature emphasized in the conversations and are not necessarily derived from particular conversational sentences.

All the exercises in *English Conversation Practice* are designed in programmed fashion: all cue words or cue sentences are presented at the left of the page and the expected responses or "answers" are given at the right. Although in strict oral procedures students will not usually refer to the text, they can, if so desired (as homework, for example), cover the right column with a strip of paper and slide the paper down, revealing each expected response after having previously made the response orally.

The situational conversations in Part 1 of the text do not have a fixed sequence. Some effort was made to put the more immediately useful and simpler conversations at the beginning of Part 1 and to space out evenly conversational groups with and without exercises;

however, the general order is only one of many possible arrangements, and it is expected that most teachers will select situational conversations in an order appropriate to their own classrooms or laboratories.

The coverage of structural and lexical features in Part 2 of the text is not comprehensive; rather it deals mainly with those aspects of the English language with which intermediate and advanced students most often have difficulty. The structural topics in Part 2 progress from those aspects of the language generally considered easy to those generally considered more difficult, and in many instances there are logical sequences of three or more topics. Again, however, there is no fixed sequence, and the teacher may wish to select topics in a somewhat different order.

Although, by grouping, the conversations in Part 2 illustrate structural or lexical items, many of the conversations can also be used for situational practice. In this connection, the Index for *English Conversation Practice* lists not only the main sections which deal with a specific situation ("Shopping" for example) but also the additional single conversations which pertain to that situation. By the same token, some of the situational conversations in Part 1 also emphasize structural points, and again, these single conversations are cross-listed in the Index.

Throughout Part 2 of the text, the symbols (?) and (??) have been used to indicate that the cue is a repetition of a preceding question supplied by the student. The single question mark indicates that the teacher is to repeat (correctly, of course) an immediately preceding simple question made by the student; the double question marks indicate the repetition of an interrogative question.

Contents

x   *Contents*

Part 2: Structural Conversations

Part 1:

Situational
Conversations

Conversation A

S1.   Hello. How are you?
S2.   Pretty well, thanks. And you?
S1.   I'm fine, thanks.
S2.   It's good to see you again.

Conversation B

S1.   Where have you been lately?
S2.   I've been busy with extra work.
S1.   I've had a lot of work to do too.
S2.   Yes. I haven't seen you for quite a while either.

Conversation C

S1.   Hello. How's everything?
S2.   Fine, thanks. How about you?
S1.   Just fine. What's new?
S2.   Nothing much.

Conversation D

S1.   I'm pleased to meet you.
S2.   The pleasure is mine.
S1.   I've heard John speak about you often.
S2.   Only good things, I hope.

Conversation E

S1.   Look who's here!
S2.   Are you surprised to see me?
S1.   Sure. I thought you were in Europe.
S2.   I was, but I got back yesterday.

Exercise 1 / Line A4 /

It's good to see you again.

nice	It's nice to see you again.
wonderful	It's wonderful to see you again.
delightful	It's delightful to see you again.
marvelous	It's marvelous to see you again.
exciting	It's exciting to see you again.

Exercise 2 / Line A4 /

It's good to see you again.

meet you	It's good to meet you again.
talk to you	It's good to talk to you again.
be with you	It's good to be with you again.
hear from you	It's good to hear from you again.
have a conversation with you	It's good to have a conversation with you again.

Exercise 3 / Line A4 /

It's good to see you again.

them	It's good to see them again.
all of you	It's good to see all of you again.
everyone	It's good to see everyone again.
John and her	It's good to see John and her again.
Mary and him	It's good to see Mary and him again.

Exercise 4 / Line A4 /

It's good to see you again.

today	It's good to see you again today.
this week	It's good to see you again this week.
during our vacation	It's good to see you again during our vacation.
so soon again	It's good to see you so soon again.
after such a long time	It's good to see you after such a long time.

Exercise 5 / Line A4 /

It's good to see you again.

wonderful	It's wonderful to see you again.
meet	It's wonderful to meet you again.
all of you	It's wonderful to meet all of you again.
so soon again	It's wonderful to meet all of you so soon again.
be with all of you	It's wonderful to be with all of you so soon again.

Exercise 6 / Line B1 /

Where have you been lately?

recently	Where have you been recently?
since June	Where have you been since June?
this past week	Where have you been this past week?
for the last month	Where have you been for the last month?
since school finished	Where have you been since school finished?

Exercise 7 / Line B1 /

Where have you been lately?

John	Where has John been lately?
all of you	Where have all of you been lately?
your friend Mary	Where has your friend Mary been lately?
John and you	Where have John and you been lately?
everyone	Where has everyone been lately?

Exercise 8 / Line B1 /

Where have you been lately?

recently	Where have you been recently?
all of you	Where have all of you been recently?
since last July	Where have all of you been since last July?
that student	Where has that student been since last July?
this past week	Where has that student been this past week?

Exercise 9 / Line B2 /

I've been busy with extra work.

tied up	I've been tied up with extra work.
with business	I've been tied up with business.
We	We've been tied up with business.
completely involved	We've been completely involved with business.
with activities	We've been completely involved with activities.

Exercise 10 / Line B3 /

I've had a lot of work to do too.

a great deal	I've had a great deal of work to do too.
finish	I've had a great deal of work to finish too.
also	I've had a great deal of work to finish also.
too much	I've had too much work to finish also.
take care of	I've had too much work to take care of also.

Exercise 11 / Line B4 /

I haven't seen you.

for quite a while	I haven't seen you for quite a while.
heard from you	I haven't heard from you for quite a while.
She	She hasn't heard from you for quite a while.
either	She hasn't heard from you for quite a while either.

Exercise 12 / Line D1 /

I'm pleased to meet you.

delighted	I'm delighted to meet you.
to make your acquaintance	I'm delighted to make your acquaintance.
happy	I'm happy to make your acquaintance.
so soon	I'm happy to make your acquaintance so soon.
to have the pleasure of meeting you	I'm happy to have the pleasure of meeting you so soon.

Exercise 13 / Line D3 /

John speaks about you.   I've heard him speak about you.
John mentions you.   I've heard him mention you.
John refers to you.   I've heard him refer to you.
John describes you.   I've heard him describe you.
John inquires about you.   I've heard him inquire about you.
John compliments you.   I've heard him compliment you.

Exercise 14 / Line E3 /

I thought you were in Europe.

the city   I thought you were in the city.
at Sandy Beach   I thought you were at Sandy Beach.
school   I thought you were at school.
the office   I thought you were at the office.
on the train to New York   I thought you were on the train to
                              New York.

Exercise 15 / Line E4 /

I got back yesterday.

two days ago   I got back two days ago.
returned   I returned two days ago.
last Thursday   I returned last Thursday.
flew home   I flew home last Thursday.
on Friday   I flew home on Friday.

Conversation A

S1. Well, I have an appointment now.
S2. I'm in quite a hurry too.
S1. Good to see you. Goodbye.
S2. Goodbye. Take care of yourself.

Conversation B

S1. I guess I'd better go now.
S2. I've got to be going now too.
S1. In that case, I'll be seeing you.
S2. So long. See you later.

Conversation C

S1. It's getting late, and I have to go now.
S2. We're sorry you have to leave.
S1. Please excuse me, won't you?
S2. Certainly. Come back soon.

Conversation D

S1. I'm glad to have met you.
S2. Thank you. It was nice to have seen you.
S1. I hope we can get together again.
S2. Yes. I'll be looking forward to it.

Conversation E

S1. I think I have to leave now.
S2. Must you go so soon?
S1. I'm afraid I really have to.
S2. Well, it was fun to get together again.

Exercise 1 / Line A1 /

I have an appointment now.

meeting	I have a meeting now.
date	I have a date now.
engagement	I have an engagement now.
class	I have a class now.

Exercise 2 / Line A1 /

I have an appointment now.

soon	I have an appointment soon.
very shortly	I have an appointment very shortly.
in a few minutes	I have an appointment in a few minutes.
an hour from now	I have an appointment an hour from now.
this evening	I have an appointment this evening.

Exercise 3 / Line A1 /

I have an appointment now.

meeting	I have a meeting now.
soon	I have a meeting soon.
engagement	I have an engagement soon.
very shortly	I have an engagement very shortly.
date	I have a date very shortly.

Exercise 4 / Line B1 /

I guess I'd better go now.

right away	I guess I'd better go right away.
very soon	I guess I'd better go very soon.
right now	I guess I'd better go right now.
in a minute or two	I guess I'd better go in a minute or two.

Exercise 5 / Lines B1 and E1 /

I think I'd better go now.

I should	I think I should go now.
I ought to	I think I ought to go now.
I have to	I think I have to go now.
I've got to	I think I've got to go now.
I must	I think I must go now.

Exercise 6 / Line B1 /

I guess I'd better go now.

think	I think I'd better go now.
I ought to	I think I ought to go now.
leave	I think I ought to leave now.
right away	I think I ought to leave right away.
should	I think I should leave right away.
quite soon	I think I should leave quite soon.

Exercise 7 / Line C1 /

It's getting late.

dark	It's getting dark.
outside	It's getting dark outside.
much colder	It's getting much colder outside.
It's been getting	It's been getting much colder outside.
cloudier	It's been getting much cloudier outside.
a lot	It's been getting a lot cloudier outside.

Exercise 8 / Line C1 /

I have to go now.

quite soon	I have to go quite soon.
must	I must go quite soon.
leave	I must leave quite soon.
in a few minutes	I must leave in a few minutes.
I've got to	I've got to leave in a few minutes.
return	I've got to return in a few minutes.

Exercise 9 / Line E4 /

It was fun to get together again.

exciting	It was exciting to get together again.
meet each other	It was exciting to meet each other again.
once more	It was exciting to meet each other once more.
talk to each other	It was exciting to talk to each other once more.
pleasant	It was pleasant to talk to each other once more.

Conversation A

S1. Do you speak English?
S2. Only a little, and not very well.
S1. Do you know many words?
S2. No, I don't. Only the important words.

Conversation B

S1. Does your brother speak English?
S2. Well, he speaks a little English.
S1. Do your sisters speak English?
S2. Yes, they do. They speak it very well.

Conversation C

S1. Can I help you?
S2. Yes. I speak only French.
S1. I'm sorry, but I don't understand French.
S2. Please find someone who speaks French.

Conversation D

S1. What's the matter?
S2. I don't speak English.
S1. Do you need some kind of help?
S2. Yes, but I can't explain it in English.

Conversation E

S1. Do you think English is easy?
S2. No, I don't.
S1. Why don't you think so?
S2. Because I don't understand it.

Exercise 1 / Lines A1 and B1 /

Do you speak English?

your brother	Does your brother speak English?
your sisters	Do your sisters speak English?
Mr. Brown	Does Mr. Brown speak English?
the lawyers	Do the lawyers speak English?
the girl	Does the girl speak English?

Exercise 2 / Lines A1 and B1 /

Do you speak English?

Greek	Do you speak Greek?
Spanish	Do you speak Spanish?
Italian	Do you speak Italian?
Portuguese	Do you speak Portuguese?

Exercise 3 / Lines A1 and B4 /

Do you speak English?

fluently	Do you speak English fluently?
rapidly	Do you speak English rapidly?
very well	Do you speak English very well?
correctly	Do you speak English correctly?

Exercise 4 / Lines A1, B1, B4 /

Do you speak English?

Japanese	Do you speak Japanese?
your brother	Does your brother speak Japanese?
fluently	Does your brother speak Japanese fluently?
Greek	Does your brother speak Greek fluently?
your sisters	Do your sisters speak Greek fluently?

Exercise 5 / Line C1 /

Can I help you?

any of you	Can I help any of you?
we	Can we help any of you?
assist	Can we assist any of you?
with anything	Can we assist any of you with anything?
you two	Can we assist you two with anything?

Exercise 6 / Line C4 /

Please find someone who speaks French.

get	Please get someone who speaks French.
bring	Please bring someone who speaks French.
ask for	Please ask for someone who speaks French.
direct me to	Please direct me to someone who speaks French.
take me to	Please take me to someone who speaks French.

Exercise 7 / Line C4 /

Please find someone who speaks French.

German	Please find someone who speaks German.
Turkish	Please find someone who speaks Turkish.
Arabic	Please find someone who speaks Arabic.
Chinese	Please find someone who speaks Chinese.

Exercise 8 / Line C4 /

Please find someone who speaks French.

bring	Please bring someone who speaks French.
Arabic	Please bring someone who speaks Arabic.
ask for	Please ask for someone who speaks Arabic.
German	Please ask for someone who speaks German.
take me to	Please take me to someone who speaks German.

Exercise 9 / Line E1 /

Do you think English is easy?

hard	Do you think English is hard?
difficult	Do you think English is difficult?
simple	Do you think English is simple?
complicated	Do you think English is complicated?

Exercise 10 / Line D2 /

I don't speak English.

The man	The man doesn't speak English.
fluently	The man doesn't speak English fluently.
The boys	The boys don't speak English fluently.
very well	The boys don't speak English very well.
understand	The boys don't understand English very well.

Conversation A

S1.   What time do you get up?
S2.   I get up about seven fifteen.
S1.   What time is breakfast at your house?
S2.   Breakfast is always at a quarter to eight.

Conversation B

S1.   What do you usually do in the afternoon?
S2.   We usually study or read.
S1.   What do you generally do over the weekend?
S2.   We generally enjoy sports and visit friends.

Conversation C

S1.   Do you ever go to museums?
S2.   I go every now and then.
S1.   What kinds of things do you like to see?
S2.   I enjoy seeing statues and old paintings.

Conversation D

S1.   Do you watch television very often?
S2.   Well, I sometimes watch it in the evening.
S1.   Did you watch television last night?
S2.   Yes, I did. I saw several good programs.

Conversation E

S1.   Do you ever listen to the radio?
S2.   Certainly. In fact, I listen practically every **night**.
S1.   What's your favorite program?
S2.   I like the Eleven O'clock Theater best of all.

Exercise 1 / Line A1 /

What time do you get up?

have breakfast	What time do you have breakfast?
leave home	What time do you leave home?
leave for work	What time do you leave for work?
return home	What time do you return home?
go to bed	What time do you go to bed?

Exercise 2 / Lines A1 and A2 /

I get up at seven fifteen.	What time do you get up?
I have breakfast about eight fifteen.	What time do you have breakfast?
I leave home at a quarter to nine.	What time do you leave home?
I go to bed about eleven o'clock.	What time do you go to bed?

Exercise 3 / Lines A1 and A3 /

What time do you have breakfast?	When do you have breakfast?
What time do you go to school?	When do you go to school?
What time do you get to the office?	When do you get to the office?
What time do you eat lunch?	When do you eat lunch?
What time do you leave for home?	When do you leave for home?

Exercise 4 / Line D1 /

Do you watch television very often?	Yes, I do.
How often do you watch television?	I watch it twice a week.
Does John watch television very often?	Yes, he does.
How often does John watch television?	He watches it twice a week.
Do the boys watch television very often?	Yes, they do.
How often do the boys watch television?	They watch it twice a week.

Exercise 5 / Line D3 /

Did you watch television last night?	Yes, I did. I watched television last night.
Did you listen to the radio last night?	Yes, I did. I listened to the radio last night.
Did you go to a movie last night?	Yes, I did. I went to a movie last night.
Did you go to the library last night?	Yes, I did. I went to the library last night.
Did you attend a concert last night?	Yes, I did. I attended a concert last night.
Did you visit a museum last night?	Yes, I did. I visited a museum last night.

Exercise 6 / Line A4 /

He's happy.	He's usually happy.
They're at home.	They're usually at home.
She's there.	She's usually there.
I'm very nervous.	I'm usually very nervous.
You're in your office.	You're usually in your office.
They're quite busy.	They're usually quite busy.
We're serious about things.	We're usually serious about things.

Exercise 7 / Lines B2 and B4 /

He writes carefully.	He usually writes carefully.
They practice at home.	They usually practice at home.
She reads popular novels.	She usually reads popular novels.
I watch television here.	I usually watch television here.
He enjoys seeing movies.	He usually enjoys seeing movies.
They leave home early.	They usually leave home early.
We get up before eight.	We usually get up before eight.

Exercise 8 / Lines A4 and B2 /

He's kind to them.	He's always kind to them.
They help her.	They always help her.
We're busy on Friday.	We're always busy on Friday.
I work extra hours.	I always work extra hours.
They're polite to us.	They're always polite to us.
He drinks black coffee.	He always drinks black coffee.
She's calm about things.	She's always calm about things.

Exercise 9 / Lines A4 and B2 /

He always works hard.	Does he always work hard?
They're always late.	Are they always late?
She's always serious.	Is she always serious?
They always speak English.	Do they always speak English?
He always writes carefully.	Does he always write carefully?
She's always patient with him.	Is she always patient with him?
They always wait for her.	Do they always wait for her?

Conversation A

S1.   When did you eat lunch today?
S2.   I ate from twelve to one.
S1.   Where did you have your lunch?
S2.   I had it at Pete's Restaurant today.

Conversation B

S1.   Did you have a good time at the party?
S2.   We had a wonderful time.
S1.   It was really a lot of fun.
S2.   We ought to have another party like that soon.

Conversation C

S1.   Did you work at home last night?
S2.   Yes. I washed the dishes and cleaned the house.
S1.   Did you do anything else?
S2.   Yes. I listened to the radio for a while.

Conversation D

S1.   Did you have a good time last night?
S2.   Yes. I had a wonderful time.
S1.   You'll probably have fun tomorrow too.
S2.   I'm sure I'll have an excellent time.

Conversation F.

S1.   Where did you go?
S2.   We went to a beautiful beach.
S1.   Did you swim in the ocean?
S2.   Yes, but we swam close to the shore!

Exercise 1 / Line A1 /

When did you eat lunch today?

have the meeting	When did you have the meeting today?
Where	Where did you have the meeting today?
meet your friends	Where did you meet your friends today?
What time	What time did you meet your friends today?
leave for home	What time did you leave for home today?

Exercise 2 / Line B3 /

It was really a lot of fun.

certainly	It was certainly a lot of fun.
a great deal of	It was certainly a great deal of fun.
definitely	It was definitely a great deal of fun.
lots of	It was definitely lots of fun.
actually	It was actually lots of fun.

Exercise 3 / Line C1 /

Did you work at home last night?

at the office	Did you work at the office last night?
yesterday	Did you work at the office yesterday?
at school	Did you work at school yesterday?
this morning	Did you work at school this morning?
at the library	Did you work at the library this morning?

Exercise 4 / Lines E3 and E4 /

Did you swim in the ocean?	Yes, we did. We swam in the ocean.
Did she go to the store?	Yes, she did. She went to the store.
Did they write in their office?	Yes, they did. They wrote in their office.
Did he read at the library?	Yes, he did. He read at the library.
Did we sing at school?	Yes, you did. You sang at school.
Did Tom and you sleep at home?	Yes, we did. We slept at home.

Conversation A

S1.   Where did you go after lunch?
S2.   I went to the public library.
S1.   Which one did you go to?
S2.   I went to the one at 42nd Street.

Conversation B

S1.   What did you do last night?
S2.   I watched television.
S1.   Where did you watch it?
S2.   I watched it here in the recreation room.

Conversation C

S1.   Was that television program interesting?
S2.   I thought it was very boring.
S1.   What did your friends think of it?
S2.   They were bored too.

Conversation D

S1.   I went to a lecture last night.
S2.   What was it about?
S1.   Society and modern art
S2.   I wish I'd gone with you.

Conversation E

S1.   We went to the movies the night before last.
S2.   What did you see?
S1.   We saw a film about cowboys and Indians.
S2.   Don't you ever get tired of those westerns?

Conversation A

S1. Where have you been?
S2. I've been to the movies.
S1. What did you see?
S2. I saw an Italian movie about life in Sicily.

Conversation B

S1. What places have you seen so far?
S2. I've been to almost all the museums.
S1. Have you gone to any parks yet?
S2. No, I haven't. I haven't had enough time for that.

Conversation C

S1. Let's meet at your house tonight.
S2. O.K. That sounds fine.
S1. I've forgotten how to get to your house.
S2. Just take the Tenth Street bus to Third Avenue.

Conversation D

S1. Let's watch television for a while.
S2. All right, but let's finish this work first.
S1. Oh, let's not do the work right now.
S2. You're just lazy, in my opinion.

Conversation E

S1. I can't hear the television set.
S2. Why don't you sit closer?
S1. I'm right beside it now.
S2. Why don't you turn up the volume?

Conversation A

S1.   Let's go the movies tonight.
S2.   Fine. I don't have anything else to do.
S1.   What would you like to see?
S2.   Why don't we look in the movie section of the newspaper?

Conversation B

S1.   Where are you going tonight?
S2.   I'm going to the political rally for Senator Smith.
S1.   Sounds interesting. Can we go with you?
S2.   Certainly. Meet me here at eight fifteen.

Conversation C

S1.   Would you like to go to the concert with me tonight?
S2.   Yes. Thank you very much.
S1.   Would you like to go at about eight o'clock?
S2.   That would be fine.

Conversation D

S1.   What are you going to do tonight?
S2.   I haven't decided yet.
S1.   Would you like to go to the movies?
S2.   Can I call you and tell you later?

Conversation E

S1.   Would you like to go to the movies tonight?
S2.   I'd rather stay home and watch television.
S1.   Are there going to be any good programs tonight?
S2.   Yes. There's going to be a good play on channel 4.

Conversation Drill A

S1. Please sit down and talk to me.
S2. Are you _____ (A) _____ ?
S1. Yes, I am. What are you doing?
S2. At the moment, I'm _____ (B) _____

(A)	(B)
typing a letter	looking for someone
painting a picture	just walking around
reading the paper	waiting for a friend
watching television	just resting a bit
listening to a record	getting ready for dinner
working on something	doing my work
writing a report	practicing English with you
solving a puzzle	relaxing for a few minutes

Conversation Drill B

S1. What do you want to do tonight?
S2. Would you like to _____ (A) _____ ?
S1. That would be nice.
S2. There's a good _____ (B) _____

(A)	(B)
watch television	program on channel 3
go bowling with us	bowling alley nearby
see a movie	show at the corner theater
listen to the radio	comedy on station WXQZ
attend a concert	orchestra at the auditorium
hear some folk music	group of musicians at the Star Club
go to a play	play which just opened
look for paintings	art gallery on Eighth Street

Conversation A

S1. I've got to go to the train station.
S2. What do you have to go for?
S1. To meet my cousin from Washington.
S2. Let me take you in my car.

Conversation B

S1. Did you get to the station on time?
S2. We did, but we were almost late.
S1. How close was it?
S2. We got on the train just as it was starting.

Conversation C

S1. Did your cousin arrive on time?
S2. No. He was an hour late.
S1. Did you meet him at the station?
S2. I was right there on the platform when the train came.

Conversation D

S1. Where's my bag?
S2. Here it is.
S1. Where's my briefcase?
S2. There it is—over there.

Conversation E

S1. Do you have your suitcases?
S2. I've got one of them with me.
S1. Where are the rest of them?
S2. I checked my two other ones at the baggage room.

Exercise 1 / Line A1 /

I've got to go to the train station.

I must	I must go to the train station.
have to	I have to go to the train station.
ought to	I ought to go to the train station.
should	I should go to the train station.
I'm supposed to	I'm supposed to go to the train station.

Exercise 2 / Line A2 /

What do you have to go for?	Why do you have to go?
What did you have to return for?	Why did you have to return?
What are you going to leave for?	Why are you going to leave?
What are you going back for?	Why are you going back?
What will you do that for?	Why will you do that?
What have you done it for?	Why have you done it?

Exercise 3 / Line A4 /

Please let me take you to your car.	Let me take you to your car.
Please let me carry your suitcase.	Let me carry your suitcase.
Please let me drive you to school.	Let me drive you to school.
Please let me help you with that.	Let me help you with that.
Please let me return the book for you.	Let me return the book for you.

Exercise 4 / Line B1 /

Did you get to the station on time?

the airport	Did you get to the airport on time?
late	Did you get to the airport late?
arrive at	Did you arrive at the airport late?
the theater	Did you arrive at the theater late?
early	Did you arrive at the theater early?

Exercise 5 / Line B4 /

We got on the train just as it was starting.

the bus	We got on the bus just as it was starting.
before it left	We got on the bus just before it left.
the airplane	We got on the airplane just before it left.
a minute or two	We got on the airplane just a minute or two early.
early	early.

Exercise 6 / Line C1 /

Did your cousin arrive on time?

aunt	Did your aunt arrive on time?
uncle	Did your uncle arrive on time?
nephew	Did your nephew arrive on time?
niece	Did your niece arrive on time?
grandmother	Did your grandmother arrive on time?

Exercise 7 / Line C1 /

Did your cousin arrive on time?

come	Did your cousin come on time?
get there	Did your cousin get there on time?
return	Did your cousin return on time?
leave	Did your cousin leave on time?
get back	Did your cousin get back on time?

Exercise 8 / Line C1 /

Did your cousin arrive on time?

late	Did your cousin arrive late?
too late	Did your cousin arrive too late?
early	Did your cousin arrive too early?
before departure	Did your cousin arrive before departure?

Exercise 9 / Line C1 /

Did your cousin arrive on time?

uncle	Did your uncle arrive on time?
get back	Did your uncle get back on time?
early	Did your uncle get back early?
nephew	Did your nephew get back early?

Exercise 10 / Line E2 /

I've got one of them with me.

my suitcases	I've got one of my suitcases with me.
a couple	I've got a couple of my suitcases with me.
my packages	I've got a couple of my packages with me.
several	I've got several of my packages with me.
my things	I've got several of my things with me.

Conversation A

S1. How do you get home every day?
S2. I take the commuter train to Westport.
S1. Isn't it rather expensive going by train?
S2. No. I buy a twenty-trip commuter ticket each month.

Conversation B

S1. Can you give me some information?
S2. You're at the right place.
S1. I want to go to Washington.
S2. The next train leaves at four thirty.

Conversation C

S1. How soon does the train leave?
S2. It leaves in ten minutes.
S1. Do I have time to check my bags?
S2. I don't think you do.

Conversation D

S1. At what time does the next train leave for the city?
S2. There's one at four and another at four forty-five.
S1. What's the fare?
S2. It's eight fifty including tax.

Conversation E

S1. How much is the fare to Miami?
S2. A hundred fifty dollars round trip.
S1. What time does the next train leave?
S2. The next one leaves at six thirty on track 31.

Conversation A

S1.   Where will you meet your friends?
S2.   I'll meet them at the airport.
S1.   When will they get there?
S2.   I don't know yet.

Conversation B

S1.   When are you meeting your friends?
S2.   I'm meeting them at eight o'clock tomorrow night.
S1.   How are they getting here?
S2.   They're coming by air.

Conversation C

S1.   Is this Southwestern Airlines?
S2.   Yes. May I help you?
S1.   Can you tell me when flight 439 will arrive?
S2.   One moment, please. I'll check.

Conversation D

S1.   All the incoming flights are listed on that board.
S2.   I see they expect Bill's flight to be twenty minutes late.
S1.   Do they have an arrival gate listed?
S2.   No. They'll probably list it about ten minutes before arrival.

Conversation E

S1.   Well! How was your trip?
S2.   It was very smooth and fast.
S1.   Could you see the mountains from the plane?
S2.   Yes. The visibility was excellent all the way.

Exercise 1 / Line A1 /

Where will you meet your friends?

see	Where will you see your friends?
find	Where will you find your friends?
wait for	Where will you wait for your friends?
take	Where will you take your friends?
drive	Where will you drive your friends?
leave	Where will you leave your friends?

Exercise 2 / Line A1 /

Where will you meet your friends?

cousin	Where will you meet your cousin?
relatives	Where will you meet your relatives?
parents	Where will you meet your parents?
brother	Where will you meet your brother?
sisters	Where will you meet your sisters?
uncle	Where did you meet your uncle?
aunt	Where did you meet your aunt?

Exercise 3 / Line A1 /

Where will you meet your friends?

parents	Where will you meet your parents?
see	Where will you see your parents?
When	When will you see your parents?
cousins	When will you see your cousins?
get together with	When will you get together with your cousins?

Exercise 4 / Line A2 /

I'll meet them at the airport.

You'll	You'll meet them at the airport.
We'll	We'll meet them at the airport.
She'll	She'll meet them at the airport.
They'll	They'll meet them at the airport.
He'll	He'll meet them at the airport.

Exercise 5 / Line A2 /

I'll meet them at the airport.

the train station	I'll meet them at the train station.
the bus station	I'll meet them at the bus station.
the terminal	I'll meet them at the terminal.
the ticket window	I'll meet them at the ticket window.
the entrance	I'll meet them at the entrance.

Exercise 6 / Line A2 /

I'll meet them at the airport.

the bus station	I'll meet them at the bus station.
We'll	We'll meet them at the bus station.
wait for	We'll wait for them at the bus station.
the ticket window	We'll wait for them at the ticket window.
She'll	She'll wait for them at the ticket window.
see	She'll see them at the ticket window.

Exercise 7 / Line B1 /

When are you meeting your friends?

seeing	When are you seeing your friends?
visitors	When are you seeing your visitors?
Where	Where are you seeing your visitors?
taking	Where are you taking your visitors?
guests	Where are you taking your guests?
Why	Why are you taking your guests?

Exercise 8 / Line B2 /

I'm meeting them at eight o'clock tomorrow night.

eight oh-five	I'm meeting them at eight oh-five tomorrow night.
eight thirty	I'm meeting them at eight thirty tomorrow night.
a quarter to nine	I'm meeting them at a quarter to nine tomorrow night.
ten to nine	I'm meeting them at ten to nine tomorrow night.
midnight	I'm meeting them at midnight tomorrow night.

Exercise 9 / Line B2 /

I'm meeting them at eight o'clock tomorrow night.

tomorrow morning	I'm meeting them at eight o'clock tomorrow morning.
Friday night	I'm meeting them at eight o'clock Friday night.
Friday morning	I'm meeting them at eight o'clock Friday morning.
tonight	I'm meeting them at eight o'clock tonight.
this morning	I'm meeting them at eight o'clock this morning.

Exercise 10 / Line B2 /

I'm meeting them at eight o'clock tomorrow night.

Tuesday night	I'm meeting them at eight o'clock Tuesday night.
we're	We're meeting them at eight o'clock Tuesday night.
eight thirty	We're meeting them at eight thirty Tuesday night.
her	We're meeting her at eight thirty Tuesday night.
morning	We're meeting her at eight thirty Tuesday morning.

Conversation A

S1. At what time does the next plane to London leave?
S2. The next one is flight 12 at eleven fifty-five.
S1. What's the next one after that?
S2. Flight 21 at one oh-five.

Conversation B

S1. How often is there a flight to Paris?
S2. We have flights to Paris every hour.
S1. Are they nonstop flights?
S2. Yes. Direct to Paris.

Conversation C

S1. Could I make a reservation for flight 10 to Tokyo?
S2. I'm sorry, but everything is taken.
S1. How about the next flight—tomorrow at two o'clock?
S2. Yes. I can give you a reservation on that.

Conversation D

S1. I'd like to check in for the flight to New York.
S2. Fine. Do you have your ticket and passport?
S1. Yes. Here's my ticket, and I'll get out my passport.
S2. Would you please put your baggage on the scales?

Conversation E

S1. How long is the flight from New York to Washington?
S2. Well, supposedly an hour, but it's sometimes longer.
S1. How often are there flights to Washington from New York?
S2. There's one every hour.

Conversation A

S1. What's a good hotel in this town?
S2. The Jefferson Hotel is good.
S1. How far is it from here?
S2. It's quite close—about four blocks.

Conversation B

S1. Where are you staying?
S2. We're staying at an excellent hotel.
S1. What's the name of the hotel?
S2. The Eastern Hotel.

Conversation C

S1. How long will you be in New York?
S2. I'll be here about two weeks.
S1. Where are you going to stay?
S2. I'm going to stay at the Madison Hotel.

Conversation D

S1. I'd like a single room, please.
S2. Do you want a room with a bath?
S1. Yes, please. Do you have one?
S2. Yes. We have one at ten dollars a day.

Conversation E

S1. I have a reservation for a room here.
S2. Yes. You're in room 341 on the third floor.
S1. Can I take the elevator over there?
S2. Yes, and turn right when you get off the elevator.

Exercise 1 / Line A1 /

What's a good restaurant in this town?

jewelry store	What's a good jewelry store in this town?
flower shop	What's a good flower shop in this town?
motel	What's a good motel in this town?
barber shop	What's a good barber shop in this town?
dress shop	What's a good dress shop in this town?
clothing store	What's a good clothing store in this town?

Exercise 2 / Line A1 /

What's a good restaurant in this town?

city	What's a good restaurant in this city?
neighborhood	What's a good restaurant in this neighborhood?
area	What's a good restaurant in this area?
district	What's a good restaurant in this district?
near here	What's a good restaurant near here?

Exercise 3 / Line A1 /

What's a good restaurant in this town?

hardware store	What's a good hardware store in this town?
area	What's a good hardware store in this area?
grocery store	What's a good grocery store in this area?
near here	What's a good grocery store near here?
jewelry store	What's a good jewelry store near here?

Exercise 4 / Line A3 /

How far is it from here?

from here to the hotel	How far is it from here to the hotel?
How many blocks	How many blocks is it from here to the hotel?
from the station	How many blocks is it from the station to the hotel?
How many miles	How many miles is it from the station to the hotel?
to the next city	How many miles is it from the station to the next city?

Exercise 5 / Line B2 /

We're staying at an excellent hotel.

living	We're living at an excellent hotel.
wonderful	We're living at a wonderful hotel.
resort	We're living at a wonderful resort.
vacationing	We're vacationing at a wonderful resort.

Exercise 6 / Line C1 /

How long will you be in New York?

at the conference	How long will you be at the conference?
How many days	How many days will you be at the conference?
in Japan	How many days will you be in Japan?
weeks	How many weeks will you be in Japan?
on the boat	How many weeks will you be on the boat?

Exercise 7 / Line C4 /

I'm going to stay at the Madison Hotel.

We're	We're going to stay at the Madison Hotel.
Central Motel	We're going to stay at the Central Motel.
She's	She's going to stay at the Central Motel.
a friend's house	She's going to stay at a friend's house.

Exercise 8 / Line D2 /

Do you want a room with a bath?

without	Do you want a room without a bath?
prefer	Do you prefer a room without a bath?
with two baths	Do you prefer a room with two baths?
a suite	Do you prefer a suite with two baths?
Would you like	Would you like a suite with two baths?

Exercise 9 / Line E2 /

You're in room 341 on the third floor.

576	You're in room 576 on the fifth floor.
777	You're in room 777 on the seventh floor.
894	You're in room 894 on the eighth floor.
1201	You're in room 1201 on the twelfth floor.

Conversation A

S1. Where's the hotel, please?
S2. It's on Main Street.
S1. Where's that?
S2. It's the next street straight ahead.

Conversation B

S1. Can you tell me where the hotel is?
S2. It's in the next block.
S1. On this side or the other side?
S2. This side. Straight ahead of you.

Conversation C

S1. I want to go to the Beachside Hotel.
S2. Do you have a map?
S1. Yes, I do. Here it is.
S2. The hotel is right there—at that intersection.

Conversation D

S1. Excuse me. I'm lost.
S2. Where do you live?
S1. I live at the Royal Hotel.
S2. The Royal Hotel is two blocks that way.

Conversation E

S1. Can you help me, please?
S2. What's the matter?
S1. Where's the Grand Hotel on this map?
S2. It's right here—right next to the train stat

Exercise 1 / Line A1 /

Where's the hotel, please?

the drugstore	Where's the drugstore, please?
the post office	Where's the post office, please?
the police station	Where's the police station, please?
the library	Where's the library, please?
the center of town	Where's the center of town, please?

Exercise 2 / Line A4 /

It's the next street straight ahead.

first	It's the first street straight ahead.
second	It's the second street straight ahead.
third	It's the third street straight ahead.
fourth	It's the fourth street straight ahead.
fifth	It's the fifth street straight ahead.

Exercise 3 / Line A4 /

It's straight ahead.

around the corner	It's around the corner.
two blocks from here	It's two blocks from here.
past the post office	It's past the post office.
near the library	It's near the library.
right after the stoplight	It's right after the stoplight.

Exercise 4 / Line B1 /

Where's the hotel?	Can you tell me where the hotel is?
Where's the drugstore?	Can you tell me where the drugstore is?
Where's the post office?	Can you tell me where the post office is?
Where's the police station?	Can you tell me where the police station is?
Where's the library?	Can you tell me where the library is?
Where's the center of town?	Can you tell me where the center of town is?

Exercise 5 / Lines B2 and C4 /

The hotel is in the next block.

on Main Street	The hotel is on Main Street.
near the police station	The hotel is near the police station.
across the street	The hotel is across the street.
three blocks away	The hotel is three blocks away.
at the intersection	The hotel is at the intersection.
by the post office	The hotel is by the post office.
on Park Avenue	The hotel is on Park Avenue.

Exercise 6 / Line C1 /

I want to go to the Beachside Hotel.

the Central Drugstore	I want to go to the Central Drugstore.
the Memorial Library	I want to go to the Memorial Library.
Penny's Department Store	I want to go to Penny's Department Store.
the Park Avenue Pharmacy	I want to go to the Park Avenue Pharmacy.
the J. F. Kennedy Airport	I want to go to the J. F. Kennedy Airport.

Exercise 7 / Line D4 /

The Royal Hotel is two blocks that way.

half a block	The Royal Hotel is half a block that way.
several blocks	The Royal Hotel is several blocks that way.
about ten blocks	The Royal Hotel is about ten blocks that way.
some distance	The Royal Hotel is some distance that way.
a five-minute walk	The Royal Hotel is a five-minute walk that way.

Exercise 8 / Line D4 /

The Royal Hotel is two blocks that way.

down the street	The Royal Hotel is two blocks down the street.
up the street	The Royal Hotel is two blocks up the street.
in that direction	The Royal Hotel is two blocks in that direction.
past the intersection	The Royal Hotel is two blocks past the intersection.
the other way	The Royal Hotel is two blocks the other way.
north of here	The Royal Hotel is two blocks north of here.

Exercise 9 / Line D4 /

The Royal Hotel is two blocks that way.

several blocks	The Royal Hotel is several blocks that way.
up the street	The Royal Hotel is several blocks up the street.
about ten blocks	The Royal Hotel is about ten blocks up the street.
in that direction	The Royal Hotel is about ten blocks in that direction.
a five-minute walk	The Royal Hotel is a five-minute walk in that direction.

Exercise 10 / Line E3 /

Where's the Grand Hotel on this map?

the Central Drugstore	Where's the Central Drugstore on this map?
the Memorial Library	Where's the Memorial Library on this map?
Main Street	Where's Main Street on this map?
the Madison Motel	Where's the Madison Motel on this map?
Greenwood Park	Where's Greenwood Park on this map?

Conversation A

S1.   Where's the airlines office?
S2.   It's near the bus terminal—the Central Terminal.
S1.   How far is that from here?
S2.   About a half a mile, I think.

Conversation B

S1.   Where's the post office?
S2.   It's three blocks that way.
S1.   What did you say?
S2.   Three blocks up that street.

Conversation C

S1.   Where's the airport?
S2.   It's north of the city.
S1.   What's the best way to get there?
S2.   Take Highway 15 to the north.

Conversation D

S1.   What street is the local library on?
S2.   I don't know.
S1.   How can I find out?
S2.   Why don't you ask a policeman?

Conversation E

S1.   Where's the nearest telephone?
S2.   There's one in that drugstore.
S1.   Do you mean that store over there?
S2.   Yes. That's the one.

Exercise 1 / Line A1 /

Where's the airlines office?

the bus terminal	Where's the bus terminal?
the train station	Where's the train station?
the airport	Where's the airport?
the local library	Where's the local library?
the nearest hospital	Where's the nearest hospital?
the next bus stop	Where's the next bus stop?

Exercise 2 / Line A4 /

It's about a half a mile from here.

a quarter of a mile	It's about a quarter of a mile from here.
three quarters of a mile	It's about three quarters of a mile from here.
2 miles	It's about 2 miles from here.
2½ miles	It's about 2½ miles from here.
a little over 3 kilometers	It's a little over 3 kilometers from here.

Exercise 3 / Line D1 /

What street is the local library on?

the post office	What street is the post office on?
the police station	What street is the police station on?
the bus depot	What street is the bus depot on?
the fire department	What street is the fire department on?
the nearest drugstore	What street is the nearest drugstore on?
the closest bus stop	What street is the closest bus stop on?

Exercise 4 / Line D3 /

How can I find out?

find that address	How can I find that address?
get that address	How can I get that address?
look up his address	How can I look up his address?
locate the library	How can I locate the library?
get to the library	How can I get to the library?

Exercise 5 / Line D3 /

How can I find out?

where it is	How can I find out where it is?
where it's located	How can I find out where it's located?
what street it's on	How can I find out what street it's on?
what district it's in	How can I find out what district it's in?
what part of the city it's in	How can I find out what part of the city it's in?
what area it's in	How can I find out what area it's in?

Exercise 6 / Line D3 /

Where is it?	How can I find out where it is?
Where's the post office?	How can I find out where the post office is?
Where's it located?	How can I find out where it's located?
What street is it on?	How can I find out what street it's on?
What street is the library on?	How can I find out what street the library is on?
What district is it in?	How can I find out what district it's in?

Exercise 7 / Line D4 /

Why don't you ask a policeman?

your friend	Why don't you ask your friend?
that man over there	Why don't you ask that man over there?
the bus driver	Why don't you ask the bus driver?
someone else	Why don't you ask someone else?
the owner of that store	Why don't you ask the owner of that store?
the conductor	Why don't you ask the conductor?

Exercise 8 / Line E1 /

Where's the nearest telephone?

drugstore	Where's the nearest drugstore?
clothing store	Where's the nearest clothing store?
grocery store	Where's the nearest grocery store?
flower shop	Where's the nearest flower shop?
dress shop	Where's the nearest dress shop?

Exercise 9 / Line E2 /

There's one in that drugstore.

near the drugstore	There's one near the drugstore.
in the hotel lobby	There's one in the hotel lobby.
on the second floor	There's one on the second floor.
down the hallway	There's one down the hallway.
on the table over there	There's one on the table over there.

Exercise 10 / Line E3 /

Do you mean that store over there?

across the street	Do you mean that store across the street?
next to the train station	Do you mean that store next to the train station?
on the corner	Do you mean that store on the corner?
opposite the airlines office	Do you mean that store opposite the airlines office?
a block down the street	Do you mean that store a block down the street?

Conversation A

S1.   What's the matter?
S2.   I need some information.
S1.   Go to that desk over there.
'S2.   Thank you very much.

Conversation B

S1.   Can you help me, please?
S2.   I'll try to.
S1.   What's the best way to get to this address?
S2.   I'm sorry, but I really don't know.

Conversation C

S1.   How can I get to that address?
S2.   You can go by taxi.
S1.   Isn't there any other way?
S2.   Yes, by bus, but it's complicated.

Conversation D

S1.   How do I get to the nearest subway station?
S2.   It's two blocks up that street.
S1.   Do you mean the street running that way?
S2.   Yes. That's the one.

Conversation E

S1.   Is this the right way to Grand Central Station?
S2.   No. You're going the wrong way.
S1.   Which way should I be going then?
S2.   It's in that direction—about six blocks.

Exercise 1 / Line A2 /

I need some information.

a little	I need a little information.
assistance	I need a little assistance.
I'd appreciate	I'd appreciate a little assistance.
with this work	I'd appreciate a little assistance with this work.
some more	I'd appreciate some more assistance with this work.

Exercise 2 / Line A3 /

Go to that desk over there.

across the room	Go to that desk across the room.
the counter	Go to the counter across the room.
Walk	Walk to the counter across the room.
opposite that door	Walk to the counter opposite that door.
the office	Walk to the office opposite that door.

Exercise 3 / Line B3 /

What's the best way to get to this address?

fastest	What's the fastest way to get to this address?
easiest	What's the easiest way to get to this address?
quickest	What's the quickest way to get to this address?
shortest	What's the shortest way to get to this address?
least difficult	What's the least difficult way to get to this address?

Exercise 4 / Line B3 /

What's the best way to get to this address?

the center of town	What's the best way to get to the center of town?
the local shopping center	What's the best way to get to the local shopping center?
the Central Hotel	What's the best way to get to the Central Hotel?
Eastern College	What's the best way to get to Eastern College?

Exercise 5 / Line B3 /

What's the best way to get to this address?

fastest	What's the fastest way to get to this address?
to the center of town	What's the fastest way to get to the center of town?
drive	What's the fastest way to drive to the center of town?
easiest	What's the easiest way to drive to the center of town?
to the Central Hotel	What's the easiest way to drive to the Central Hotel?

Exercise 6 / Line C2 /

You can go by taxi.

ought to	You ought to go by taxi.
by bus	You ought to go by bus.
there	You ought to go there by bus.
should	You should go there by bus.
on the train	You should go there on the train.

Exercise 7 / Line D1 /

How do I get to the subway station?

the bus depot	How do I get to the bus depot?
reach	How do I reach the bus depot?
Highway 16	How do I reach Highway 16?
find	How do I find Highway 16?
the baggage room	How do I find the baggage room?

Exercise 8 / Line D2 /

It's two blocks up that street.

a few	It's a few blocks up that street.
down	It's a few blocks down that street.
a short distance	It's a short distance down that street.
along the highway	It's a short distance along the highway.
several miles	It's several miles along the highway.

Conversation A

S1. Pardon me. Where's the Central Theater?
S2. It's in the next block—straight ahead.
S1. Thank you very much.
S2. That's all right.

Conversation B

S1. Where's the National Department Store?
S2. It's downtown—on Brown Street.
S1. Do you know the exact address?
S2. Yes. It's 521 Brown Street.

Conversation C

S1. Can you tell me where the library is located?
S2. Yes. Do you see that church down the street?
S1. Yes. It's quite easy to see with such a tall spire.
S2. Just turn left there and walk three blocks.

Conversation D

S1. Are the instructions too complicated for you?
S2. Well, would you mind repeating them?
S1. I'd be glad to.
S2. I'd like to write them down this time.

Conversation E

S1. Can you tell me where the station is?
S2. Turn right and go four blocks.
S1. Would you mind repeating that?
S2. I'd be glad to.

Conversation A

S1.   Where do I get the downtown bus?
S2.   Walk straight ahead one block.
S1.   Thanks very much.
S2.   Don't mention it.

Conversation B

S1.   Where does the bus stop?
S2.   At the next corner.
S1.   Does it go downtown?
S2.   Only the number 5 bus goes downtown.

Conversation C

S1.   Are there many bus stops along this street?
S2.   Yes, there are. There are quite a few.
S1.   Are they located at the corners?
S2.   Most of them are, but a few aren't.

Conversation D

S1.   How do I get to the station?
S2.   Take the bus at the next corner.
S1.   Do you know which bus I take?
S2.   Watch for number 32.

Conversation E

S1.   How much is the fare on this bus?
S2.   It's fifteen cents.
S1.   Do I give the money to you?
S2.   No. Just drop it in this machine.

Conversation A

S1. Does this bus go into the city?
S2. Yes. Where do you want to go?
S1. I want to go to Harbor Heights.
S2. This is the right bus then.

Conversation B

S1. Does this bus go as far as Washington Square?
S2. No. You'll have to transfer.
S1. Where can I do it?
S2. You can get the Washington Square bus at the next corner.

Conversation C

S1. Is this where I get off the bus?
S2. No. Not here—at the next stop.
S1. Can I catch a taxi right there?
S2. Yes. There's a taxi stand right by the bus stop.

Conversation D

S1. Excuse me, but how do I get to this address?
S2. Get off the bus at Water Street and Main.
S1. Thanks very much for your help.
S2. Don't mention it.

Conversation E

S1. Is West Street the next stop?
S2. I'm sorry, but I didn't understand you.
S1. Does the bus stop at West Street next?
S2. Yes. Right at the next corner.

Conversation A

S1.   Where are you going now?
S2.   To the hotel.
S1.   Are you going by bus or by taxi?
S2.   Probably by taxi if I can get one.

Conversation B

S1.   I need a taxi.
S2.   The taxis are by the entrance.
S1.   Thank you very much.
S2.   You're welcome.

Conversation C

S1.   Is this taxi taken?
S2.   No. Where are you going?
S1.   I'm going to the University Student Center.
S2.   O.K. I know right where it is.

Conversation D

S1.   How much is the fare?
S2.   Two dollars and fifty cents.
S1.   Here. Keep the change.
S2.   Thank you very much.

Conversation E

S1.   It's raining very hard right now.
S2.   Why don't we get a taxi?
S1.   That's a good idea.
S2.   Now, I only hope we can find one.

Conversation A

S1. Are you taking a trip today?
S2. Yes. We're going to Boston.
S1. It's a good day for the trip.
S2. I'm glad the sun is shining.

Conversation B

S1. How far is it from here to the coast?
S2. It's about 250 miles.
S1. How long does it take to get there by car?
S2. It takes about five hours.

Conversation C

S1. How far is it to the next gas station?
S2. There's one two miles from here.
S1. Is there a place to eat there?
S2. Yes. There's a restaurant next to the station.

Conversation D

S1. What's the best way to Ocean City.
S2. The superhighway, but it's also the longest way.
S1. How much longer is it that way?
S2. About 10 or 12 miles.

Conversation E

S1. Are they going by way of North Plains?
S2. No. They aren't taking that route.
S1. How are they traveling then?
S2. They're driving directly to Ocean City.

Conversation A

S1. I have to take a trip by air next week.
S2. Do you like to fly?
S1. I don't know because I've never flown before.
S2. You'll probably like it very much.

Conversation B

S1. I have to go home next week.
S2. How will you go—by car?
S1. I'll probably go by air.
S2. You'll get there very fast then.

Conversation C

S1. Are you going on a trip next Saturday?
S2. Yes. We're going to Boston.
S1. Are you flying or going by train?
S2. We're traveling by car.

Conversation D

S1. How will you travel to Los Angeles?
S2. We'll go by plane.
S1. How long will it take?
S2. It'll take about five or six hours to get there.

Conversation E

S1. What time will you leave your house?
S2. I'll leave around seven thirty.
S1. How are you going to go—by train or by bus?
S2. Neither. I'm going to drive.

Conversation Drill A

S1. Excuse me. Where's ___(A)___ ?
S2. It's ___(B)___
S1. Thank you for the help.
S2. That's all right.

(A)	(B)
the rest room	down the hall
the post office	around the corner
the bus terminal	in the next block
the ticket office	by the main entrance

Conversation Drill B

S1. Where's the ___(A)___ ?
S2. It's on this floor.
S1. How can I get there from here?
S2. ___(B)___

(A)	(B)
reception desk	Turn left right over there.
main office	Walk straight ahead.
cafeteria	Go in the second door on the right.
cashier's window	Just walk to the end of this hall.

Conversation Drill C

S1. How do I get to the train station?
S2. Turn left ___(A)___
S1. How far is it ___(B)___ ?
S2. It's about a quarter of a mile.

(A)	(B)
at the second stoplight	to the stoplight
in the center of town	to the center
at the next intersection	to the intersection
at Main Street	to Main Street
by the bus depot	to the depot

Conversation A

S1.   What time do you have?
S2.   It's ten o'clock sharp.
S1.   Thanks a lot.
S2.   Don't mention it.

Conversation B

S1.   What's the time?
S2.   It's almost eight.
S1.   Do you have the exact time?
S2.   Yes, it's two minutes to eight.

Conversation C

S1.   Excuse me. What time is it?
S2.   It's a quarter of two.
S1.   I guess my watch is slow then.
S2.   Well, I know mine isn't fast.

Conversation D

S1.   What time is it right now?
S2.   It's five twenty-five.
S1.   I've got five thirty-five.
S2.   You're ten minutes fast then.

Conversation E

S1.   Do you have the correct time?
S2.   Yes. It's two minutes to three.
S1.   Are you sure your watch is right?
S2.   It may be a few minutes slow.

Exercise 1 / Line B2 /

It's almost eight thirty.

about	It's about eight thirty.
just about	It's just about eight thirty.
around	It's around eight thirty.
close to	It's close to eight thirty.
nearly	It's nearly eight thirty.

Exercise 2 / Line D2 /

It's five o'clock.	Is it five o'clock?
It's five fifteen.	Is it five fifteen?
It's a quarter after five.	Is it a quarter after five?
It's twenty after five.	Is it twenty after five?
It's five twenty-five.	Is it five twenty-five?
It's five thirty.	Is it five thirty?
It's twenty to six.	Is it twenty to six?
It's five forty-five.	Is it five forty-five?
It's a quarter to six.	Is it a quarter to six?
It's ten to six.	Is it ten to six?

Exercise 3 / Lines D2, D3, D4 /

It's five o'clock, but I've got five ten.	You're ten minutes fast then.
It's five o'clock, but I've got ten to five.	You're ten minutes slow then.
It's five fifteen, but I've got five twelve.	You're three minutes slow then.
It's five twenty-five, but I've got five thirty.	You're five minutes fast then.
It's five to six, but I've got five forty-five.	You're ten minutes fast then.

Exercise 4 / Line E3 /

Is your watch right?	Are you sure your watch is right?
Is your watch wrong?	Are you sure your watch is wrong?
Is your watch slow?	Are you sure your watch is slow?
Is your watch fast?	Are you sure your watch is fast?
's your watch correct?	Are you sure your watch is correct?

Conversation A

S1. What time is it now?
S2. I don't have my watch on right now.
S1. Is there a clock around here?
S2. There's one in the next room.

Conversation B

S1. Do you have the right time?
S2. I was just going to ask you the same question.
S1. My watch has stopped.
S2. I forgot to wear mine.

Conversation C

S1. Do you have any idea of the time?
S2. I don't know exactly, but it's after nine.
S1. It was nine o'clock when I got here.
S2. Well, I'm sorry I can't help you.

Conversation D

S1. At what time is the meeting?
S2. Eight o'clock.
S1. Be there at eight o'clock sharp, then.
S2. I'll try to get there before eight.

Conversation E

S1. How often does this station give the news?
S2. Every hour on the hour.
S1. When do they announce the weather?
S2. Ten minutes to and ten minutes after the hour.

Exercise 1 / Line A2 /

I don't have my watch on right now.

coat	I don't have my coat on right now.
hat	I don't have my hat on right now.
shoes	I don't have my shoes on right now.
sweater	I don't have my sweater on right now.
wristwatch	I don't have my wristwatch on right now.

Exercise 2 / Line A3 /

Is there a clock around here?

in this room	Is there a clock in this room?
in the other room	Is there a clock in the other room?
in this building	Is there a clock in this building?
on the table	Is there a clock on the table?
on the wall	Is there a clock on the wall?
near this room	Is there a clock near this room?

Exercise 3 / Line A3 /

Is there a clock around here?

a big clock	Is there a big clock around here?
an electric clock	Is there an electric clock around here?
a wall clock	Is there a wall clock around here?
any clocks	Are there any clocks around here?
any wall clocks	Are there any wall clocks around here?

Exercise 4 / Line A3 /

Is there a clock around here?

in the other room	Is there a clock in the other room?
electric	Is there an electric clock in the other room?
in this building	Is there an electric clock in this building?
clocks	Are there electric clocks in this building?
any	Are there any electric clocks in this building?
around here	Are there any electric clocks around here?

Exercise 5 / *Line B1* /

Do you have the time?

right	Do you have the right time?
have any idea of	Do you have any idea of the right time?
know the right time	Do you know the right time?
correct	Do you know the correct time?
right now	Do you know the correct time right now?
exact	Do you know the exact time right now?

Exercise 6 / *Line B2* /

I was just going to ask you the same question.

the time	I was just going to ask you the time.
tell	I was just going to tell you the time.
preparing	I was just preparing to tell you the time.
it's twelve o'clock	I was just preparing to tell you it's twelve o'clock.
a quarter to one	I was just preparing to tell you it's a quarter to one.

Exercise 7 / *Line C3* /

It was nine o'clock when I got here.

about	It was about nine o'clock when I got here.
three twenty	It was about three twenty when I got here.
arrived	It was about three twenty when I arrived here.
at the office	It was about three twenty when I arrived at the office.
sharp	It was three twenty sharp when I arrived at the office.

Exercise 8 / *Line D1* /

At what time is the meeting?

the lecture	At what time is the lecture?
the conference	At what time is the conference?
the party	At what time is the party?
the concert	At what time is the concert?
the football game	At what time is the football game?
the program	At what time is the program?

Exercise 9 / Line D1 /

At what time is the meeting?

At what time of the day	At what time of the day is the meeting?
On what day	On what day is the meeting?
On what day of the week	On what day of the week is the meeting?
In what month	In what month is the meeting?
In what month of the year	In what month of the year is the meeting?

Exercise 10 / Line D1 /

At what time is the meeting?

the lecture	At what time is the lecture?
At what time of the day	At what time of the day is the lecture?
the conference	At what time of the day is the conference?
On what day	On what day is the conference?
the party	On what day is the party?

Exercise 11 / Line D1 /

The meeting is at eight.	At what time is the meeting?
At what time is the meeting?	It's at eight.
The lecture is on Tuesday.	On what day is the lecture?
On what day is the lecture?	It's on Tuesday.
The conference is in June.	In what month is the conference?
In what month is the conference?	It's in June.
The party is at seven thirty.	At what time is the party?
At what time is the party?	It's at seven thirty.
The football game is on Friday.	On what day is the football game?
Oh what day is the football game?	It's on Friday.

Exercise 12 / Line D3 /

Be there at eight o'clock sharp, then.

at eight thirty	Be there at eight thirty sharp, then.
exactly at noon	Be there exactly at noon, then.
before three o'clock	Be there before three o'clock, then.
around ten fifteen	Be there around ten fifteen, then.
about four thirty or five	Be there about four thirty or five, then.

Exercise 13 / Line E1 /

This station gives the news.	How often does this station give the news?
This station announces the weather.	How often does this station announce the weather?
This station gives concerts.	How often does this station give concerts?
This station announces traffic conditions.	How often does this station announce traffic conditions?
This station gives plays.	How often does this station give plays?

Exercise 14 / Line E3 /

This station gives the news.	When does this station give the news?
This station announces the weather.	When does this station announce the weather?
This station gives concerts.	When does this station give concerts?
This station announces traffic conditions.	When does this station announce traffic conditions?
This station gives plays.	When does this station give plays?

Conversation A

S1. When is your first class?
S2. At ten after nine.
S1. When do you get back here, then?
S2. About ten to twelve.

Conversation B

S1. Alice will be back in ten or fifteen minutes.
S2. How long has she been out of the office?
S1. She's been out since ten o'clock.
S2. Then she's been out for an hour or more.

Conversation C

S1. I got to the cafeteria around noon.
S2. I was there, but I didn't see you.
S1. I think I left a few minutes after twelve.
S2. I must have just missed you, then.

Conversation D

S1. Our friends will meet us here.
S2. Will they come here right after lunch?
S1. No. They won't be here until three o'clock.
S2. Then I'll come a little before three.

Conversation E

S1. Let's call Mary.
S2. Let's not call her right now.
S1. Maybe this is a bad time to call.
S2. Let's wait until seven or seven thirty.

Conversation A

S1. I'm afraid we're going to be late.
S2. How much time is there left?
S1. We've got about thirty or forty minutes.
S2. That should be plenty of time.

Conversation B

S1. Whom are you waiting for?
S2. We're waiting for our friend.
S1. What are you looking so angry for?
S2. Because she's twenty minutes late already.

Conversation C

S1. Aren't we going to be late for the meeting?
S2. No. I think we'll be on time.
S1. Well, I want to be there in time to get a good seat.
S2. The meeting doesn't start for another twenty minutes.

Conversation D

S1. Isn't Harry here yet?
S2. Here he comes now.
S1. Eight forty-five. Late as usual.
S2. Well, we can still get to school on time.

Conversation E

S1. Are we late or not?
S2. No. In fact we're early according to my watch.
S1. Hadn't we better go inside?
S2. All right, but we're really about a half an hour early.

Conversation Drill A

S1. Could you tell me the time, please?
S2. Certainly. It's ___(A)___ .
S1. My watch says ___(B)___ .
S2. Then your watch is ___(C)___ .

(A)	(B)	(C)
3:10	five after three	five minutes slow
4:15	four twenty	five minutes fast
12:45	eighteen to one	three minutes slow
9:05	nine oh-five	right on time
1:30	one o'clock	half an hour off
7:55	five after seven	ten minutes off
2:00	one o'clock	an hour behind
8:45	twelve fifteen	not operating

Conversation Drill B

S1. Where's your brother?
S2. I think he s ___(A)___ now.
S1. Will he come back here ___(B)___ ?
S2. Yes. I think so.

(A)	(B)
at the store	very soon
at work	before five o'clock
at his office	at the usual time
at school	within an hour
at the library	in the afternoon
at church	at six fifteen
at the factory	in time for dinner
at home	in an hour or so

Conversation A

S1. When does February have twenty-nine days?
S2. In leap year.
S1. How often is there a leap year?
S2. Every fourth year.

Conversation B

S1. How many days are there in leap year?
S2. There are three hundred and sixty-six.
S1. How many weeks are there in a year?
S2. There are fifty-two weeks in a year.

Conversation C

S1. What are the seasons in this country?
S2. Winter, spring, summer, and fall.
S1. How many months are there in a season?
S2. There are three months in each season.

Conversation D

S1. Today is the first day of spring.
S2. I didn't realize it.
S1 Aren't you glad it's here?
S2. I'm always glad when winter is over.

Conversation E

S1. The weather is perfect today, isn't it?
S2. Yes. I like this season of the year very much.
S1. Most people like this season best of all, don't they?
S2. Well, I'm sure a lot of people do.

Exercise 1 / Lines B1–B4, C3, C4 /

How many days are there in a year?	There are three hundred and sixty-five.
How many weeks are there in a year?	There are fifty-two.
How many months are there in a year?	There are twelve.
How many seasons are there in a year?	There are four.
How many months are there in a season?	There are three.
How many days are there in a week?	There are seven.
How many days are there in June?	There are thirty.
How many days are there in October?	There are thirty-one.
How many years are there in a decade?	There are ten.
How many years are there in a century?	There are one hundred.

Exercise 2 / Line D1 /

Today is the first day of spring.

Yesterday	Yesterday was the first day of spring.
Tomorrow	Tomorrow will be the first day of spring.
Last Friday	Last Friday was the first day of spring.
Next Thursday	Next Thursday will be the first day of spring.
This coming Monday	This coming Monday will be the first day of spring.

Exercise 3 / Line D1 /

Today is the first day of spring.

summer	Today is the first day of summer.
winter	Today is the first day of winter.
September	Today is the first day of September.
the new year	Today is the first day of the new year.
our summer vacation	Today is the first day of our summer vacation.

Exercise 4 / Line D4 /

When is winter over?	It's over about March twenty-first.
Are you glad then?	I'm always glad when winter is over.
When is spring over?	It's over about June twenty-first.
Are you sorry then?	I'm always sorry when spring is over.
When is summer over?	It's over about September twenty-first.
Are you glad then?	I'm always glad when summer is over.
When is fall over?	It's over about December twenty-first.
Are you sorry then?	I'm always sorry when fall is over.

Exercise 5 / Line E1 /

The weather is perfect today, isn't it?

terrible	The weather is terrible today, isn't it?
wonderful	The weather is wonderful today, isn't it?
awful	The weather is awful today, isn't it?
unusual	The weather is unusual today, isn't it?
unusually nice	The weather is unusually nice today, isn't it?

Exercise 6 / Line E1 /

Today is very warm, isn't it?	Today isn't very warm, is it?
Today is very cold, isn't it?	Today isn't very cold, is it?
Today is very hot, isn't it?	Today isn't very hot, is it?
Today is very cool, isn't it?	Today isn't very cool, is it?
Today is very humid, isn't it?	Today isn't very humid, is it?
Today is very clear, isn't it?	Today isn't very clear, is it?

Exercise 7 / Line E3 /

Most people like this season best of all, don't they?

A lot of people	A lot of people like this season best of all, don't they?
Some people	Some people like this season best of all, don't they?
A few people	A few people like this season best of all, don't they?
Few people	Few people like this season best of all, do they?
Not many people	Not many people like this season best of all, do they?

Conversation Drill A

S1. What day is today?
S2. It's _____(A)_____ today.
S1. What's the date?
S2. It's _____(B)_____ .

(A)	(B)
Tuesday	March fifteenth
Thursday	October twenty-first
Wednesday	the third of August
Sunday	September thirtieth
Friday	the fourteenth of December

Conversation Drill B

S1. I know about the seasons in the United States now.
S2. Then when does _____(A)_____ begin?
S1. It begins in _____(B)_____ .
S2. That's right. It begins in _____(B)_____ .

(A)	(B)
spring	March
fall	September
summer	June
winter	December

Conversation Drill C

S1. I'm familiar with the seasons already.
S2. What are the names of the _____(A)_____ months then?
S1. They're _____(B)_____ .
S2. Right. _____(B)_____ are the _____(A)_____ months.

(A)	(B)
summer	June, July, and August
spring	March, April, and May
winter	December, January, and February
fall	September, October, and November

Conversation A

S1.   What floor is your apartment on?
S2.   It's on the third floor.
S1.   Is the building a walk-up?
S2.   No. It has a small elevator.

Conversation B

S1.   How large is your apartment?
S2.   It has four and a half rooms.
S1.   Then you have two bedrooms.
S2.   Right. A living room, a kitchen, two bedrooms, and a bath.

Conversation C

S1.   Is this your apartment?
S2.   Yes, it is.
S1.   How many bedrooms do you have?
S2.   Two big ones and one small one.

Conversation D

S1.   What's a cooperative apartment?
S2.   In a cooperative, you actually buy the apartment.
S1.   Just as you would buy a house?
S2.   Yes. Then you only pay maintenance costs each month.

Conversation E

S1.   Do you like your new apartment?
S2.   Yes. I like the service in the building, too.
S1.   Are there doormen and guards?
S2.   Yes, and the building is close to the shopping areas.

Conversation A

S1. How much did you pay for your house?
S2. It cost eighteen thousand dollars, and we've spent another two thousand on repairs.
S1. Did you have trouble getting a mortgage?
S2. No. We paid four thousand dollars, and the bank lent us the rest.

Conversation B

S1. Do you prefer a one-story or a two-story house?
S2. One-story, I think.
S1. I do too, because there are no stairs to climb.
S2. But one-story houses take more land.

Conversation C

S1. Your house is very large.
S2. Yes. We have enough room for guests now.
S1. Our house is too small.
S2. You don't have enough room, do you?

Conversation D

S1. Where's the bathroom?
S2. The bathroom is opposite that big bedroom.
S1. Is this the kitchen?
S2. Yes. It's a big kitchen, isn't it?

Conversation E

S1. I enjoy having a house in the suburbs.
S2. It's wonderful to have trees and a big yard.
S1. The children can play outside most of the time.
S2. And it's so much cleaner here than in the city.

34. *Using the Telephone* / *Conversations*

Conversation A

S1. Could you give me the number of the Best Bag Company?
S2. Is that in the city or in the suburbs?
S1. In the city. On Tenth Street.
S2. Just a moment, please.

Conversation B

S1. What's the telephone number of Pan-Eastern Airways?
S2. Just a moment, please.
S1. Thank you, operator.
S2. That number is Hillside 6-7600.

Conversation C

S1. I'd like to speak to Bob, please.
S2. What number are you calling?
S1. M-U-one-four-three-seven-six.
S2. Sorry. You've got the wrong number.

Conversation D

S1. May I speak to the director, please?
S2. Who's calling, please?
S1. Tell him it's his friend from California.
S2. Just a moment, please.

Conversation E

S1. I'd like to speak to Mr. Bush, please.
S2. May I ask who's calling, please?
S1. Tell him it's his assistant.
S2. Please hold the line while I see if he's in.

Conversation A

S1. Do you wish some assistance?
S2. Yes. How much is that pen?
S1. This one or that one?
S2. The one next to the black one.

Conversation B

S1. May I help you?
S2. Yes. I'd like to look at pens.
S1. Certainly. Fountain pens or ball-point pens?
S2. I'm looking for a good fountain pen.

Conversation C

S1. Could you help me, please?
S2. What can I do for you?
S1. Could I look at the wristwatch in this case?
S2. Just one moment, please, while I get the key.

Conversation D

S1. Hello. Are you waited on?
S2. No. I'd like a ream of typing paper, please.
S1. Will there be anything else?
S2. No. I believe that's all, thank you.

Conversation E

S1. Is someone helping you?
S2. I beg your pardon?
S1. Could I help you with anything?
S2. No, thanks. Someone is already waiting on me.

Exercise 1 / Line A1 /

Do you wish some assistance?

want	Do you want some assistance?
help	Do you want some help?
Would you like	Would you like some help?
advice	Would you like some advice?
care for	Would you care for some advice?

Exercise 2 / Line A2 /

How much is that pen?	How much does that pen cost?
How much are those dishes?	How much do those dishes cost?
How much is that briefcase?	How much does that briefcase cost?
How much are those gloves?	How much do those gloves cost?
How much is that alarm clock?	How much does that alarm clock cost?
How much are those glasses?	How much do those glasses cost?

Exercise 3 / Line A2 /

How much does that pen cost?	What does that pen cost?
How much do those dishes cost?	What do those dishes cost?
How much does that briefcase cost?	What does that briefcase cost?
How much do those gloves cost?	What do those gloves cost?
How much does that alarm clock cost?	What does that alarm clock cost?
How much do those glasses cost?	What do those glasses cost?

Exercise 4 / Line A2 /

How much is that pen?	What does that pen cost?
How much are those glasses?	What do those glasses cost?
How much is that billfold?	What does that billfold cost?
How much are those two ash-trays?	What do those two ashtrays cost?
How much is that small vase?	What does that small vase cost?

Exercise 5 / Line A4 /

I mean the one next to the black one.

beside	I mean the one beside the black one.
close to	I mean the one close to the black one.
behind	I mean the one behind the black one.
in front of	I mean the one in front of the black one.
opposite	I mean the one opposite the black one.
near	I mean the one near the black one.
under	I mean the one under the black one.

Exercise 6 / Line B2 /

I'd like to look at pens.	May I look at your pens?
I'd like to look at cameras.	May I look at your cameras?
I'd like to look at billfolds.	May I look at your billfolds?
I'd like to look at watches.	May I look at your watches?
I'd like to look at suitcases.	May I look at your suitcases?
I'd like to look at suits.	May I look at your suits?
I'd like to look at overcoats.	May I look at your overcoats?

Exercise 7 / Line B4 /

I'm looking for a good fountain pen.

expensive	I'm looking for an expensive fountain pen.
wristwatch	I'm looking for an expensive wristwatch.
cheap	I'm looking for a cheap wristwatch.
camera	I'm looking for a cheap camera.
small	I'm looking for a small camera.
practical	I'm looking for a practical camera.

Exercise 8 / Line C1 /

Could you help me, please?

assist	Could you assist me, please?
Would	Would you assist me, please?
advise	Would you advise me, please?
Can	Can you advise me, please?
wait on me	Can you wait on me, please?
take care of	Can you take care of me, please?

Exercise 9 / Line C3 /

Could I look at the wristwatch in this case?

gold pen	Could I look at the gold pen in this case?
in the black box	Could I look at the gold pen in the black box?
small camera	Could I look at the small camera in the black box?
on the shelf	Could I look at the small camera on the shelf?
black leather billfold	Could I look at the black leather billfold on the shelf?

Exercise 10 / Line D2 /

I'd like a ream of typing paper, please.

a pad of drawing paper	I'd like a pad of drawing paper, please.
a packet of lined paper	I'd like a packet of lined paper, please.
a bottle of ink	I'd like a bottle of ink, please.
a box of paper clips	I'd like a box of paper clips, please.
a box of stationery	I'd like a box of stationery, please.

Conversation A

S1. What store did you go to yesterday?
S2. I went to the Central Department Store.
S1. Do they have a good variety of things to choose from?
S2. They have lots to choose from, but it's all very expensive.

Conversation B

S1. What were you doing at that department store?
S2. I was shopping for a new suitcase.
S1. What was your friend doing there?
S2. She was trying to find a coat.

Conversation C

S1. I have to go shopping.
S2. Do you know what you're going to buy?
S1. Not yet, but I hope to after shopping.
S2. I hate to go shopping, but I guess it's necessary.

Conversation D

S1. What time do the stores close?
S2. Most of them close at six o'clock.
S1. Do we still have time to go shopping?
S2. Yes. It's only four fifteen now.

Conversation E

S1. It seems I always have to buy a lot of things.
S2. It always seems that way to me too.
S1. I always need so many little things.
S2. They add up to a lot of money, don't they?

Conversation A

S1.   Where do you do your shopping?
S2.   I usually start at the Central Department Store.
S1.   What do you think of their selection?
S2.   They have a good selection, and their prices are low, too.

Conversation B

S1.   They're having a big sale at the Greenfield Shopping Center.
S2.   Anything in particular on sale?
S1.   Well, they advertised linens and house furnishings.
S2.   I suppose there'll be crowds of people in the store.

Conversation C

S1.   I spent the afternoon shopping for clothes.
S2.   How did you make out?
S1.   Well, I found an excellent raincoat, and I bought some shoes.
S2.   That reminds me that I have to go shopping soon.

Conversation D

S1.   Where did you buy your coat?
S2.   I bought it at the Fifth Avenue Store—but a long time ago.
S1.   About how much did it cost?
S2.   At the moment, I've forgotten how much it cost.

Conversation E

S1.   Why did you choose the green one?
S2.   To tell the truth, I really didn't have much choice in my size.
S1.   Excuse my asking, but how much did you pay for it?
S2.   It was on sale, and I paid only forty-five dollars.

Conversation A

S1. What would you like to see?
S2. I'd like to see your overcoats, please.
S1. What kind of overcoats would you like to see?
S2. I'd like to see your winter overcoats—probably wool.

Conversation B

S1. I'd like to look at your sweaters, if I could.
S2. Certainly. Any particular style?
S1. Could I see some of the new styles, please?
S2. Of course. Please step right this way.

Conversation C

S1. I'm interested in seeing your summer suits.
S2. What color did you have in mind?
S1. White, or some light color, I think.
S2. Step over to this other room with me, would you please?

Conversation D

S1. That jacket you have on now seems to fit you very well.
S2. What kind of material is this?
S1. It's a mixture—cotton and wool.
S2. I'm not sure it's heavy enough for the fall weather.

Conversation E

S1. Here's a very popular kind of sport coat—the most recent thing.
S2. I notice there isn't much padding in the shoulders.
S1. No. It has a natural shoulder line.
S2. I like the narrow lapels and the stitching on them.

Conversation A

S1. How much does this pen cost?
S2. I beg your pardon.
S1. How much is this pen?
S2. It's four dollars and fifty cents.

Conversation B

S1. How much is this leather billfold?
S2. It's five twenty-five.
S1. Does that include the tax?
S2. It's five forty-four including tax.

Conversation C

S1. This briefcase costs five fifty.
S2. That's fine. I'll take it.
S1. Will there be anything else?
S2. I don't believe so, thank you.

Conversation D

S1. We're having a sale on leather goods today.
S2. Are office supplies on sale too?
S1. Yes. Prices have been reduced from 20 to 40 percent.
S2. I notice the sale prices are marked in red ink.

Conversation E

S1. How much are these things all together?
S2. Let's see. That'll be twenty-one fifty.
S1. I'd like to charge them to my account, please.
S2. Fine. Could you give me your name and address?

Exercise 1 / Lines A1, B1, C1 /

How much does this pen cost?   It cost two dollars.
How much do these bookends cost?   They cost two dollars.
How much does that notebook cost?   It costs two dollars.
How much do those brushes cost?   They cost two dollars.
How much does this stationery cost?   It costs two dollars.

Exercise 2 / Lines A4, B4, C1 /

It's four fifty-nine.   It costs four dollars and fifty-nine cents.
They're two fifty.   They cost two dollars and fifty cents.
It's seven eighty-five.   It costs seven dollars and eighty-five cents.

They're nine sixty-seven.   They cost nine dollars and sixty-seven cents.

They're twelve seventy.   They cost twelve dollars and seventy cents.

It's twenty-five fifty.   It costs twenty-five dollars and fifty cents.

Exercise 3 / Lines A4, B4, C1 /

What's ten fifty plus forty-nine?   It's ten ninety-nine.
What's two seventy-five plus ten?   It's two eighty-five.
What's six thirty-nine plus twenty?   It's six fifty-nine.
What's three eighty plus eighteen?   It's three ninety-eight.
What's sixty-nine plus eight?   It's seventy seven.
What's one twenty plus eight twenty?   It's nine forty.

Exercise 4 / Line D1 /

We're having a sale on leather goods today.

summer clothing   We're having a sale on summer clothing today.
home furniture   We're having a sale on home furniture today.
kitchen items   We're having a sale on kitchen items today.
household supplies   We're having a sale on household supplies today.
dinnerware   We're having a sale on dinnerware today.

Conversation A

S1. How much are your potatoes, sir?
S2. Twenty-five cents a pound.
S1. How much would five pounds cost?
S2. Five pounds would be a dollar and a quarter.

Conversation B

S1. What does that gold pin cost?
S2. It's twenty-one dollars plus tax.
S1. How much for the small one next to it?
S2. That one costs twelve fifty.

Conversation C

S1. What's the regular price for that refrigerator?
S2. The list price is two hundred forty.
S1. Are you selling it at a discount?
S2. Yes. The discount price is one ninety-nine.

Conversation D

S1. What are you asking for that antique mirror?
S2. That's one hundred fifty dollars.
S1. Isn't that rather expensive?
S2. Not really. Mirrors of that type are quite rare.

Conversation E

S1. What would it cost to have this chair repaired?
S2. I'd estimate sixty to seventy dollars.
S1. How much would it cost to replace it with a new one?
S2. Probably around a hundred dollars.

Conversation A

S1. Can you come along with us tomorrow?
S2. I think I can borrow enough money to go.
S1. Why couldn't you go last Thursday?
S2. Because I couldn't afford it.

Conversation B

S1. How much money do you have?
S2. Not very much.
S1. Do you have many dollar bills?
S2. Not very many, I'm afraid.

Conversation C

S1. You look upset about something.
S2. I think I've lost my money.
S1. Oh, that's what's bothering you.
S2. It's a good reason to be upset, isn't it?

Conversation D

S1. Are you sure you lost your money?
S2. I'm sure I did.
S1. Would you please look again?
S2. I will, but I'm sure it's not here.

Conversation E

S1. How many pennies did you have in your bank?
S2. I had exactly five hundred of them.
S1. What did you do with them?
S2. I put them in rolls of fifty pennies each.

Conversation A

S1. Have you made very much money this year?
S2. Not an awful lot.
S1. How hard have you tried?
S2. Not as hard as I could have, I'm afraid.

Conversation B

S1. How much did you make this week?
S2. Sixty-two dollars.
S1. Is that your take-home pay?
S2. Yes, it is.

Conversation C

S1. I've got to pay a lot of bills.
S2. And I've got to pay my rent today.
S1. Money goes very fast these days, doesn't it?
S2. It certainly does.

Conversation D

S1. Did you sell your car?
S2. Yes. I sold it to my friend Bob.
S1. Did you put the money in the bank?
S2. I deposited part of it and spent the rest.

Conversation E

S1. Do you have an account at that bank?
S2. I've got a special checking account.
S1. How much do you have to keep in the account?
S2. There's no minimum.

Conversation A

S1. Could you lend me a dollar until tomorrow?
S2. I can if you have change for a five.
S1. I wish I did, but I don't.
S2. Well, we can get it changed easily.

Conversation B

S1. I need about ten dollars.
S2. What do you need it for?
S1. I need it for books and supplies.
S2. O.K. I'll lend it to you.

Conversation C

S1. Could I borrow some money from you for a few days?
S2. How much do you need?
S1. Could you spare four or five dollars?
S2. Yes, but I'll need the money myself before next week.

Conversation D

S1. What did you need the money for yesterday?
S2. I wanted it for a new suit.
S1. Did you get the money?
S2. Yes. I borrowed it from a friend.

Conversation E

S1. How much change have you got?
S2. Two quarters, two nickels, and a dime.
S1. That's not enough to change this dollar bill.
S2. I'll lend you all of this change if you want it.

Conversation A

S1. Please give me nine five-cent stamps.
S2. Here they are.
S1. How much is that?
S2. Forty-five cents.

Conversation B

S1. I'd like to mail this package.
S2. How do you want to send it?
S1. By regular mail.
S2. That'll be eighty-nine cents.

Conversation C

S1. I want to send this letter special delivery.
S2. All right. I'll weigh it.
S1. How much will it cost to go that way?
S2. It'll cost fifty-five cents.

Conversation D

S1. What's the fastest way to send this package?
S2. Airmail special, but it'll be expensive.
S1. How much will it cost to send it airmail special?
S2. Just a moment. I'll weigh it and see.

Conversation E

S1. Do you sell envelopes here?
S2. Only envelopes with stamps printed on them.
S1. Can I buy books of stamps here too?
S2. Yes, you can.

Conversation A

S1.   How much are the potatoes?
S2.   I beg your pardon.
S1.   How much do the potatoes cost?
S2.   Fifteen cents a pound.

Conversation B

S1.   I'd like a bag of onions and a jar of olives.
S2.   Do you need fruit—apples, lemons, plums?
S1.   Perhaps a box of cherries and a bunch of grapes.
S2.   I'll put all this in a box with your other groceries.

Conversation C

S1.   I forgot to buy some rice.
S2.   How much do you want?
S1.   Would you please get me two pounds?
S2.   All right. A two-pound bag.

Conversation D

S1.   Don't you need milk or cream?
S2.   Yes. Let's get a pint of cream and two quarts of milk.
S1.   We can get a two-quart container.
S2.   Let's get some sour cream too.

Conversation E

S1.   Please give me two bottles of milk.
S2.   All of our milk is in cartons.
S1.   Cartons are all right, but I prefer bottles.
S2.   Cartons are more convenient, and there's a deposit on bottles.

Conversation A

S1. What do you call a big grocery store like this?
S2. It's called a "supermarket."
S1. It's convenient to see everything and pick out what you want.
S2. Having these carts to put things in is convenient too.

Conversation B

S1. How about fish tonight—salmon, tuna fish, trout?
S2. I notice the clams and oysters are fresh today.
S1. That sounds very good.
S2. Let's also get a pork roast or turkey for tomorrow.

Conversation C

S1. Now we have sugar, salt, pepper, and flour.
S2. We also need mustard, vinegar, and cinnamon.
S1. I'll get those while you get the cabbage and celery.
S2. Fine. I'll meet you at the check-out counter.

Conversation D

S1. Would you please get me a bag of sugar?
S2. Do you want two or five pounds?
S1. A two-pound bag will be all right.
S2. OK. I'll meet you at the canned-food counter.

Conversation E

S1. How many eggs should we get?
S2. Two dozen should be enough.
S1. How much butter do you think we need?
S2. One pound is enough, don't you think?

Conversation A

S1. Are you Dr. Taylor?
S2. No. That tall fellow is Dr. Taylor.
S1. Do you mean the one over there with glasses?
S2. Yes. The one with brown hair.

Conversation B

S1. Who's that very handsome man?
S2. What did you say?
S1. Do you know who that man over there is?
S2. If you mean the thin, rather dark man, that's Mr. Walker.

Conversation C

S1. Do you recognize the girl talking to Mr. Brown?
S2. Of course I know the girl he's talking to.
S1. Well then, whom is he talking to?
S2. That's Dorothy Jones, Mary's good friend.

Conversation D

S1. What's that man's name—the man that's holding the briefcase?
S2. I know, but I can't remember it right now.
S1. Where does he come from—Greece or Turkey perhaps?
S2. One of the two, I think.

Conversation E

S1. Do you know the man over there by the door?
S2. I do, but I can't remember his name at the moment.
S1. Isn't he a famous musician?
S2. He's either a musician or a painter.

Exercise 1 / Line A1 /

Are you Mrs. Brown?	No, I'm not. I'm not Mrs. Brown.
Are you a teacher?	No, I'm not. I'm not a teacher.
Are you lawyers?	No, we aren't. We aren't lawyers.
Are you doctors?	No, we aren't. We aren't doctors.
Are you an artist?	No, I'm not. I'm not an artist.

Exercise 2 / Line A2 /

That tall fellow is Mr. Taylor.

short	That short fellow is Mr. Taylor.
with brown hair	That short fellow with brown hair is Mr. Taylor.
gray	That short fellow with gray hair is Mr. Taylor.
thin fellow	That thin fellow with gray hair is Mr. Taylor.
That fellow with glasses	That fellow with glasses is Mr. Taylor.

Exercise 3 / Lines B2 and B3 /

Who's that man?	Do you know who that man is?
Who are those men?	Do you know who those men are?
Who's that woman?	Do you know who that woman is?
Who are those women?	Do you know who those women are?
Who's that thin fellow?	Do you know who that thin fellow is?
Who are those two girls?	Do you know who those two girls are?

Exercise 4 / Line C1 /

Do you recognize the girl talking to Mr. Brown?

standing by the door	Do you recognize the girl standing by the door?
walking across the room	Do you recognize the girl walking across the room?
carrying the blue purse	Do you recognize the girl carrying the blue purse?
wearing the yellow dress	Do you recognize the girl wearing the yellow dress?
shaking hands with Mr. Brown	Do you recognize the girl shaking hands with Mr. Brown?

Exercise 5 / Line C2 /

He's talking to a girl.	I know the girl he's talking to.
He's looking at a girl.	I know the girl he's looking at.
He's speaking about a girl.	I know the girl he's speaking about.
He's standing beside a girl.	I know the girl he's standing beside.
He's leaving with a girl.	I know the girl he's leaving with.
He's listening to a girl.	I know the girl he's listening to.

Exercise 6 / Line C3 /

He's talking to a girl.	Whom is he talking to?
He's listening to a girl.	Whom is he listening to?
He's looking at a girl.	Whom is he looking at?
He's standing beside a girl.	Whom is he standing beside?
He's speaking about a girl.	Whom is he speaking about?
He's leaving with a girl.	Whom is he leaving with?

Exercise 7 / Line C3 /

Whom is he speaking about?	Do you know whom he's speaking about?
Whom is he leaving with?	Do you know whom he's leaving with?
Whom is he looking at?	Do you know whom he's looking at?
Whom is he listening to?	Do you know whom he's listening to?
Whom is he standing beside?	Do you know whom he's standing beside?

Exercise 8 / Lines E3 and E4 /

He plays music for people.	He's a musician.
He types things.	He's a typist.
He runs a farm.	He's a farmer.
He instructs students.	He's an instructor.
He takes photographs.	He's a photographer.
He sings songs professionally.	He's a professional singer.
He translates things.	He's a translator.
He collects stamps.	He's a stamp collector.
He organizes groups for the union.	He's a union organizer.
He analyzes legal matters.	He's a legal analyst.
He supervises factory workers.	He's a factory supervisor.

Conversation A

S1. How old is your son?
S2. He's seventeen years old.
S1. Is your daughter older or younger than your son?
S2. Younger. She's only fifteen.

Conversation B

S1. Have you got many relatives here?
S2. Yes. An aunt and an uncle and four grandparents.
S1. Do your aunt and uncle have children?
S2. Yes. I have three cousins—two boys and a girl.

Conversation C

S1. Do you have a picture of your family?
S2. Yes, I've got one right here.
S1. You have a very nice family.
S2. Thank you.

Conversation D

S1. Jim looks like his father.
S2. Do you and your father look alike?
S1. There's a little resemblance but not much.
S2. I don't look like anyone at all in my family.

Conversation E

S1. How's your family?
S2. They're all fine, thanks.
S1. Are your niece and nephew still here?
S2. Yes, they are. They're still visiting me.

Conversation A

S1. Which house is your house?
S2. Ours is the last one on the block.
S1. Is yours the red one or the blue one?
S2. The blue one on the right side of the street.

Conversation B

S1. What's the name of that book John referred to?
S2. It's slipped my mind for the moment.
S1. Who did he say was the author?
S2. Some man whose name starts with an *m*.

Conversation C

S1. Which one of these are you going to choose?
S2. I like the red one with the blue stripes.
S1. The one over there with black edges is nice too.
S2. But the one we looked at first may be the best choice.

Conversation D

S1. The car over there by the streetlight is John's.
S2. Which one do you mean—the old one or the new red one?
S1. Neither. I mean the streetlight on your left.
S2. Oh. Then the one with the convertible top must be his.

Conversation E

S1. What's the name of that thing with the strange shape?
S2. I beg your pardon.
S1. Can you tell me what the name of that thing over there is?
S2. Sorry. I don't know myself.

Exercise 1 / Lines A1–A4 /

Our house is the last one.	Ours is the last one.
Their house is the last one.	Theirs is the last one.
His house is the last one.	His is the last one.
My house is the last one.	Mine is the last one.
Her house is the last one.	Hers is the last one.

Exercise 2 / Lines A1–A4 /

His books are the red ones.	His are the red ones.
Their books are the red ones.	Theirs are the red ones.
Your books are the red ones.	Yours are the red ones.
Her books are the red ones.	Hers are the red ones.
My books are the red ones.	Mine are the red ones.

Exercise 3 / Lines A2 and A4 /

Ours is the last one on the right side.

left	Ours is the last one on the left side.
next to last	Ours is the next to last one on the left side.
Theirs	Theirs is the next to last one on the left side.
first	Theirs is the first one on the left side.
other	Theirs is the first one on the other side.

Exercise 4 / Lines A1, C1, C4, D2 /

Which of them is the best?

the most practical	Which of them is the most practical?
the cheapest	Which of them is the cheapest?
the most expensive	Which of them is the most expensive?
the prettiest	Which of them is the prettiest?
the most stylish	Which of them is the most stylish?

Exercise 5 / Line B1 /

What's the name of that book he referred to?

inquired about	What's the name of that book he inquired about?
commented on	What's the name of that book he commented on?
spoke about	What's the name of that book he spoke about?
objected to	What's the name of that book he objected to?

Exercise 6 / Line C1 /

Are you going to choose one?	Which one are you going to choose?
Have you chosen one?	Which one have you chosen?
Did you choose one?	Which one did you choose?
Should you choose one?	Which one should you choose?
Will you choose one?	Which one will you choose?
Had you chosen one?	Which one had you chosen?

Exercise 7 / Line C2 /

I like the one with blue stripes.	I like the one that has blue stripes.
I like the one with black edges.	I like the one that has black edges.
I like the one with green sides.	I like the one that has green sides.
I like the one with yellow squares.	I like the one that has yellow squares.
I like the one with orange flowers.	I like the one that has orange flowers.

Exercise 8 / Line C4 /

We looked at that one.	The one we looked at may be the best.
We examined that one.	The one we examined may be the best.
We talked about that one.	The one we talked about may be the best.
We chose that one.	The one we chose may be the best.
We picked out that one.	The one we picked out may be the best.
We selected that one.	The one we selected may be the best

Exercise 9 / Line E3 /

Can you tell me what the name of that is?

Can you guess	Can you guess what the name of that is?
Can't you guess	Can't you guess what the name of that is?
Do you know	Do you know what the name of that is?
Don't you know	Don't you know what the name of that is?

Conversation A

S1. Are you writing a letter?
S2. Yes. I'm writing to my family.
S1. Do you write letters very often?
S2. Yes. I write five or six letters a week.

Conversation B

S1. Do you write letters very often?
S2. No. I hate to write letters.
S1. It takes a lot of time.
S2. It sure does.

Conversation C

S1. Did Robert get a letter?
S2. Yes. He got one yesterday.
S1. Does he get many letters?
S2. Yes. He gets some every day.

Conversation D

S1. Charles wrote me a long letter.
S2. When did he write to you?
S1. He sent the letter to me about a week ago.
S2. He hasn't even sent me a postcard yet!

Conversation E

S1. We wrote to Mary's sister last week.
S2. Has she written to you yet?
S1. No, she hasn't.
S2. She wrote to me a few days ago.

Conversation A

S1. Have you written to your brother yet?
S2. Yes, but I haven't mailed the letter yet.
S1. I went to the post office half an hour ago.
S2. Why didn't you tell me?

Conversation B

S1. Did your friend in San Francisco write to you?
S2. Yes. I got a letter from her on Thursday.
S1. What did she have to say?
S2. She said the city was interesting and pretty.

Conversation C

S1. Did you write a reply to Peter's letter?
S2. Yes. I wrote one on Friday.
S1. Did you mention his last letter to you?
S2. Yes. I said I'd enjoyed his letter a lot.

Conversation D

S1. What are you writing?
S2. I'm writing a thank-you note to the Smiths.
S1. What are you doing that for?
S2. I had dinner with them, and it's customary to write a thank-you note.

Conversation E

S1. I wrote a letter to them applying for a job.
S2. Was it hard to write your letter of application?
S1. Yes. I wanted to sound modest but also mention my qualifications.
S2. It's always hard to write about yourself.

Conversation A

S1.   Have you got any change?
S2.   What do you need?
S1.   I need change for a quarter.
S2.   Here are two dimes and five pennies.

Conversation B

S1.   Can you change this five-dollar bill?
S2.   I'm sorry. I don't have change.
S1.   What should I do?
S2.   Go to the cashier's desk.

Conversation C

S1.   Can you change this ten-dollar bill?
S2.   How do you want it?
S1.   A five and five ones, please.
S2.   Here you are.

Conversation D

S1.   Do you have change for a dollar bill?
S2.   Just a minute, and I'll see.
S1.   I need some quarters.
S2.   Yes. I can change it and give you two quarters.

Conversation E

S1.   This is a change machine.
S2.   Do you really get money from it?
S1.   Sure. Just put a fifty-cent piece in that slot.
S2.   It works! I've got a quarter, two dimes, and a nickel.

Exercise 1 / Line D1 /

Do you have change for a dime?

a quarter	Do you have change for a quarter?
a half dollar	Do you have change for a half dollar?
a dollar	Do you have change for a dollar?
a five-dollar bill	Do you have change for a five-dollar bill?

Exercise 2 / Lines A1 and D1 /

Have you got change for a dime?

a half dollar	Have you got change for a half dollar?
a quarter	Have you got change for a quarter?
a five-dollar bill	Have you got change for a five-dollar bill?
a fifty-cent piece	Have you got change for a fifty-cent piece?

Exercise 3 / Lines A1 and D1 /

Have you got change for a dime?	I wonder if you've got change for a dime.
Have you got change for a quarter?	I wonder if you've got change for a quarter.
Have you got change for fifty cents?	I wonder if you've got change for fifty cents.
Have you got change for a five?	I wonder if you've got change for a five.

Exercise 4 / Lines B1 and C1 /

Can you change this dime?

fifty-cent piece	Can you change this fifty-cent piece?
quarter	Can you change this quarter?
ten-dollar bill	Can you change this ten-dollar bill?
half dollar	Can you change this half dollar?
five-dollar bill	Can you change this five-dollar bill?

Exercise 5 / Lines A3 and A4 /

I need change for a nickel.	Here are five pennies.
I need change for a dime.	Here are ten pennies.
I need change for a quarter.	Here are twenty-five pennies.
I need change for a half dollar.	Here are fifty pennies.
I need change for a dollar.	Here are one hundred pennies.

Conversation Drill A

S1. I understand the American money system well.
S2. Then how many ___(A)___ are there in a ___(B)___ ?
S1. There are ___(C)___ , aren't there?
S2. That's exactly right. There are ___(C)___ .

(A)	(B)	(C)
cents	nickel	five
cents	dime	ten
nickels	dime	two
cents	quarter	twenty-five
nickels	quarter	five
quarters	half dollar	two
dimes	half dollar	five
quarters	dollar	four
nickels	dollar	twenty

Conversation Drill B

S1. What do you need today?
S2. I'd like ___(A)___
S1. Today ___(B)___
S2. That'll be all right, thanks.

(A)	(B)
a pound of butter	butter is 65¢ a pound
a quart of milk	milk is 38¢ a quart
a loaf of bread	bread is 20¢ a loaf
a jar of jelly	jelly is 36¢ a jar
a can of tuna fish	tuna is 85¢ a can
a box of cookies	cookies are 42¢ a box
a pint of cream	cream is 41¢ a pint
a dozen eggs	eggs are 87¢ a dozen

Conversation A

S1. Is it raining now?
S2. Yes, it is. It's raining very hard.
S1. Does it rain very much in this area?
S2. Yes. It rains a lot in the spring and fall.

Conversation B

S1. How's the weather?
S2. It's raining outside now.
S1. Is it raining very hard?
S2. No, it isn't. It's just sprinkling.

Conversation C

S1. What's the weather like outside?
S2. I think it's going to rain.
S1. It was nice a few hours ago.
S2. It was beautiful, wasn't it?

Conversation D

S1. How's the weather today?
S2. It's quite cold and damp.
S1. How are the winters here in general?
S2. They're usually rather mild.

Conversation E

S1. Is it raining outside now?
S2. Yes, it is, and it's quite cold.
S1. I think I'll stay home today.
S2. I certainly wish I could too.

Exercise 1 / Line B2 /

It's raining outside now.

sprinkling	It's sprinkling outside now.
snowing	It's snowing outside now.
hailing	It's hailing outside now.
getting windy	It's getting windy outside now.

Exercise 2 / Lines A1 and B2 /

It's raining now.

yesterday	It rained yesterday.
tomorrow	It's going to rain tomorrow.
several times this week	It's rained several times this week.
a great deal in this season	It rains a great deal in this season.

Exercise 3 / Lines A1 and B2 /

It's raining now.	Is it raining now?
It rained yesterday.	Did it rain yesterday?
It's going to rain tomorrow.	Is it going to rain tomorrow?
It's rained many times this week.	Has it rained many times this week?
It rains a great deal in this season.	Does it rain a great deal in this season?

Exercise 4 / Line D2 /

It's quite cold and damp.

cloudy and gray	It's quite cloudy and gray.
windy and cold	It's quite windy and cold.
warm and humid	It's quite warm and humid.
hot and sticky	It's quite hot and sticky.

Exercise 5 / Line D4 /

The winters are usually rather mild here.

generally	The winters are generally rather mild here.
very wet	The winters are generally very wet here.
the summers	The summers are generally very wet here.
almost always	The summers are almost always very wet here.

Conversation A

S1. It was hot yesterday.
S2. But it's quite cool today.
S1. Yes. I'm wearing a sweater under my coat.
S2. I'm going to put on a jacket.

Conversation B

S1. It's freezing today!
S2. Yes. It's worse than yesterday.
S1. How cold is it?
S2. t's ten below.

Conversation C

S1. What cold weather this is!
S2. It certainly is.
S1. What's the temperature?
S2. It's five above.

Conversation D

S1. You've seen a hurricane, haven't you?
S2. Once, a long time ago.
S1. Does it ever snow in your country?
S2. Only a few times a year.

Conversation E

S1. Do you like the weather in this part of the country?
S2. Not really, but I'm adjusted to it now.
S1. Is the weather different in your part of the country?
S2. Yes. It never gets as cold there as it does here.

Exercise 1 / Lines A1 and A2 /

It was hot yesterday.   It *was* quite hot, wasn't it?
It was cold yesterday.   It *was* quite cold, wasn't it?
It was warm yesterday.   It *was* quite warm, wasn't it
It was cool yesterday.   It *was* quite cool, wasn't it?
It was chilly yesterday.   It *was* quite chilly, wasn't it?
It was damp yesterday.   It *was* quite damp, wasn't it?

Exercise 2 / Line A4 /

I'm going to put on a sweater.

a wool shirt   I'm going to put on a wool shirt.
a jacket   I'm going to put on a jacket.
gloves   I'm going to put on gloves.
an overcoat   I'm going to put on an overcoat.
overshoes   I'm going to put on overshoes.

Exercise 3 / Line B2 /

It's worse than yesterday.

better   It's better than yesterday.
hotter   It's hotter than yesterday.
colder   It's colder than yesterday.
warmer   It's warmer than yesterday.
cooler   It's cooler than yesterday.

Exercise 4 / Line B2 /

It's worse than yesterday.   It's the worst day in a long time.
It's hotter than yesterday.   It's the hottest day in a long time.
It's colder than yesterday.   It's the coldest day in a long time.
It's warmer than yesterday.   It's the warmest day in a long time.
It's cooler than yesterday.   It's the coolest day in a long time.

Exercise 5 / Line C1 /

What cold weather this is!

humid   What humid weather this is!
hot   What hot weather this is!
cloudy   What cloudy weather this is!
damp   What damp weather this is!
sticky   What sticky weather this is!

Conversation A

S1. It's a nice day, isn't it?
S2. Yes. It's warm and sunny for a change.
S1. I like this kind of weather.
S2. I guess everyone does.

Conversation B

S1. It's a little windy today.
S2. I don't mind the wind.
S1. The sun certainly feels good.
S2. Especially after all that bad weather last week.

Conversation C

S1. The weather is good today.
S2. It's a little too warm for me.
S1. This kind of weather is good for the farmers.
S2. But I'm not a farmer.

Conversation D

S1. I wonder what the weather is going to be like tomorrow.
S2. The paper says it's going to be fair and sunny.
S1. Let's listen to the weather report on the radio.
S2. That's a good idea.

Conversation E

S1. It's very warm and sticky today.
S2. It's so humid! I wish it would rain.
S1. A good rain would cool things off a little.
S2. We need some rain to make things green.

Exercise 1 / Line A1 /

It's a nice day, isn't it?

fine	It's a fine day, isn't it?
beautiful	It's a beautiful day, isn't it?
wonderful	It's a wonderful day, isn't it?
terrible	It's a terrible day, isn't it?
awful	It's an awful day, isn't it?

Exercise 2 / Lines A1 and C1 /

The weather is good today.	It *is* good, isn't it?
The weather is fine today.	It *is* fine, isn't it?
The weather is nice today.	It *is* nice, isn't it?
The weather is wonderful today.	It *is* wonderful, isn't it?
The weather is beautiful today.	It *is* beautiful, isn't it?
The weather is unusual today.	It *is* unusual, isn't it?

Exercise 3 / Lines A2 and E1 /

It's warm and sunny for a change.

damp and chilly	It's damp and chilly for a change.
cloudy and gray	It's cloudy and gray for a change.
hot and hazy	It's hot and hazy for a change.
cool and clear	It's cool and clear for a change.
windy and cold	It's windy and cold for a change.

Exercise 4 / Lines B1 and C2 /

It's warm today.	It's a little too warm for me.
It's chilly today.	It's a little too chilly for me.
It's damp today.	It's a little too damp for me.
It's windy today.	It's a little too windy for me.
It's cool today.	It's a little too cool for me.
It's hot today.	It's a little too hot for me.

Exercise 5 / Line D1 /

Is it cold outside?	I wonder if it's cold outside.
Is it cloudy outside?	I wonder if it's cloudy outside.
Is it warm outside?	I wonder if it's warm outside.
Is it chilly outside?	I wonder if it's chilly outside.
Is it windy outside?	I wonder if it's windy outside.

Conversation Drill A

S1. What's the weather like outside?

S2. Right at the moment, _____(A)_____

S1. This morning, it was _____(B)_____

S2. And tonight, it'll probably change again.

(A)	(B)
it's raining a little	a little cloudy
the wind is blowing hard	kind of damp
it's pouring	rather hazy
the sun is shining	quite cool
it's clearing up a little	very dark
the rain is stopping	windy and cold
it's getting foggy	really quite clear
the snow is getting heavy	sunny and warm

Conversation Drill B

S1. The weather isn't very good today, is it?

S2. No, it certainly isn't.

S1. It's _____(A)_____

S2. It always seems _____(B)_____ .

(A)	(B)
too damp and chilly	colder when it's damp
getting kind of hazy	gloomy when it's hazy
very cloudy and gray	gloomier when it's cloudy
getting even more humid	uncomfortable when it's humid
quite windy and cold	worse when it's windy
getting icy on the roads	strange when there's ice on the roads
too hot and sticky	hotter when it's humid
becoming rather dark	depressing when it's so dark

Conversation A

S1.   Were you at home last night?
S2.   No, but I was at home the night before last.
S1.   Will you be at home tomorrow night?
S2.   No, but I'll be at home the next night.

Conversation B

S1.   Didn't your friends leave the week before last?
S2.   Right. They left just two weeks ago.
S1.   Will they get back next week?
S2.   Yes. According to them, they'll arrive a week from today.

Conversation C

S1.   Did Mary get back last week?
S2.   Yes. She got back on Thursday.
S1.   How long was she away?
S2.   She was out of town for ten days.

Conversation D

S1.   When did George arrive in town?
S2.   He flew in last Thursday afternoon.
S1.   John has been here since last Thursday too.
S2.   Both of them plan to leave the day after tomorrow.

Conversation E

S1.   How long have you been here?
S2.   I've been here for two months.
S1.   How often do you get here?
S2.   I get to this city about twice a year

Exercise 1 / Line A1 /

Were you at home yesterday?

yesterday afternoon	Were you at home yesterday afternoon?
last night	Were you at home last night?
the day before yesterday	Were you at home the day before yesterday?
the night before last	Were you at home the night before last?
two nights ago	Were you at home two nights ago?
last Thursday night	Were you at home last Thursday night?

Exercise 2 / Line A3 /

Will you be at home tomorrow?

tomorrow afternoon	Will you be at home tomorrow afternoon?
tomorrow night	Will you be at home tomorrow night?
the day after tomorrow	Will you be at home the day after tomorrow?
a week from today	Will you be at home a week from today?
next Friday night	Will you be at home next Friday night?

Exercise 3 / Lines B1 and C1 /

Didn't your friends get back last week?

last Monday	Didn't your friends get back last Monday?
a week ago	Didn't your friends get back a week ago?
a week ago today	Didn't your friends get back a week ago today?
two weeks ago	Didn't your friends get back two weeks ago?
the week before last	Didn't your friends get back the week before last?

Exercise 4 / Line B3 /

Will they get back next week?

next Tuesday	Will they get back next Tuesday?
a week from now	Will they get back a week from now?
a week from today	Will they get back a week from today?
two weeks from now	Will they get back two weeks from now?
the week after next	Will they get back the week after next?

Exercise 5 / Line C4 /

She was out of town for ten days.

a week	She was out of town for a week.
a week and a half	She was out of town for a week and a half.
several weeks	She was out of town for several weeks.
quite a while	She was out of town for quite a while.
a couple of months	She was out of town for a couple of months.

Exercise 6

My brother met them on Tuesday.

at two o'clock	My brother met them at two o'clock.
see	My brother saw them at two o'clock.
last night	My brother saw them last night.
telephone	My brother telephoned them last night.
an hour ago	My brother telephoned them an hour ago.
consult	My brother consulted them an hour ago.
in the evening	My brother consulted them in the evening.
advise	My brother advised them in the evening.
yesterday morning	My brother advised them yesterday morning.
help	My brother helped them yesterday morning.
last Tuesday	My brother helped them last Tuesday.
pay	My brother paid them last Tuesday.
the day before last	My brother paid them the day before last.

Exercise 7

They're going to help you tonight.

in the spring	They're going to help you in the spring.
instruct	They're going to instruct you in the spring.
tomorrow night	They're going to instruct you tomorrow night.
visit	They're going to visit you tomorrow night.
on October twentieth	They're going to visit you on October twentieth.
He	He's going to visit you on October twentieth.
next week	He's going to visit you next week.
assist	He's going to assist you next week.
the day after tomorrow	He's going to assist you the day after tomorrow.
meet	He's going to meet you the day after tomorrow.
We	We're going to meet you the day after tomorrow.
invite	We're going to invite you the day after tomorrow.
in March	We're going to invite you in March.
supervise	We're going to supervise you in March.
on March eighteenth	We're going to supervise you on March eighteenth.

Conversation Drill A

S1. When will Mr. Brown arrive in the city?
S2. He'll arrive here ___(A)___ .
S1. His wife got here ___(B)___ .
S2. I didn't know that.

(A)	(B)
next month	last month
on the twenty-fifth	in August
a week from now	a week ago
at four o'clock	at twelve fifteen
the day after tomorrow	the day before yesterday
two hours from now	two hours ago
in the evening	during the afternoon
tomorrow night	last night

Conversation Drill B

S1. How long will you be away?
S2. Probably ___(A)___ .
S1. Have you made all the arrangements?
S2. Yes. I'm going to leave ___(B)___ .

(A)	(B)
until the summer	before the holiday
for six months	on the twenty-fifth
up to November	during the spring
twenty or twenty-one days	in September
six months or more	on September eighteenth
a long time	after the ceremony
until July fourth	next week
not for long	sometime next month.

Conversation A

S1. How long have you worked in this office?
S2. I've worked here since March.
S1. How long ago did you finish school?
S2. I finished school three years ago.

Conversation B

S1. Didn't you study English in school?
S2. Yes, but that was many years ago.
S1. How many years ago was it?
S2. At least six or seven.

Conversation C

S1. Did your friends arrive here in the fall?
S2. Yes, they did. They got here in October.
S1. Do you know the exact date they arrived?
S2. Yes, I do. They got back on October eleventh.

Conversation D

S1. Have you been living here very long?
S2. No. I've only been here since last spring.
S1. Are you going to stay until Christmas?
S2. No. I'll probably leave for France in a month or two.

Conversation E

S1. I worked on my report until midnight last night.
S2. Do you expect to finish the work by tomorrow night?
S1. Well, I certainly can't finish it before that time.
S2. You'd better get someone to help you for a few hours today
   then.

Exercise 1 / Line A2 /

I've worked here since March.

March fifteenth	I've worked here since March fifteenth.
last April	I've worked here since last April.
last fall	I've worked here since last fall.
1964	I've worked here since 1964.
the holidays	I've worked here since the holidays.

Exercise 2 / Line A2 /

I've worked here for six months.

several years	I've worked here for several years.
more than a year	I've worked here for more than a year.
a month and a half	I've worked here for a month and a half.
quite a while	I've worked here for quite a while.

Exercise 3 / Line A2 /

I worked in London for four years.

a year and a half	I worked in London for a year and a half.
eighteen weeks	I worked in London for eighteen weeks.
several months	I worked in London for several months.
a long time	I worked in London for a long time.

Exercise 4 / Line A2 /

I started to work here two months ago.

a couple of years	I started to work here a couple of years ago.
several weeks	I started to work here several weeks ago.
quite a while	I started to work here quite a while ago.
a long time	I started to work here a long time ago.

Exercise 5 / Line D3 /

I'm going to stay here until August tenth.

for two weeks	I'm going to stay here for two weeks.
until June or July	I'm going to stay here until June or July.
for a month or two	I'm going to stay here for a month or two.
until school starts	I'm going to stay here until school starts.

Exercise 6

He's worked there since September.

two months	He's worked there for two months.
1963	He's worked there since 1963.
two years	He's worked there for two years.
January first	He's worked there since January first.
several hours	He's worked there for several hours.
last winter	He's worked there since last winter.
ten o'clock	He's worked there since ten o'clock.
December	He's worked there since December.
three months	He's worked there for three months.
July 18, 1964	He's worked there since July 18, 1964.
half an hour	He's worked there for half an hour.
a long time	He's worked there for a long time.
this morning	He's worked there since this morning.
some time	He's worked there for some time.
quite a while	He's worked there for quite a while.

Exercise 7

They studied there for ten weeks.

October	They studied there in October.
one year	They studied there for one year.
1965	They studied there in 1965.
two hours	They studied there for two hours.
the spring	They studied there in the spring.
a month	They studied there for a month.
several weeks	They studied there for several weeks.
the winter	They studied there in the winter.
1963 and '64	They studied there in 1963 and '64.
an hour or two	They studied there for an hour or two.
the fall semester	They studied there in the fall semester.
a whole month	They studied there for a whole month.
a short time	They studied there for a short time.
June and July	They studied there in June and July.
quite a while	They studied there for quite a while.

Conversation Drill A

S1.   I'm leaving the country very soon.

S2.   You're coming back ___(A)___, aren't you?

S1.   I'll be back ___(B)___

S2.   Well, relax and enjoy your vacation!

(A)	(B)
next fall	in September or October
in the spring	at the end of May
before the winter	on December fifteenth
after the holidays	sometime before April first

Conversation Drill B

S1.   What would you like to do?

S2.   I'd like to ___(A)___ .

S1.   I would too, but I can't.

S2.   Maybe we can ___(B)___ .

(A)	(B)
go shopping	go Friday or Saturday
see a movie	see one tomorrow night
go for a walk	go for one in the morning
go swimming	go tomorrow or the next day
ride over to John's	do it some other day

Conversation Drill C

S1.   Could I help you?

S2.   How long will it take ___(A)___ ?

S1.   How soon do you need it?

S2.   I was hoping to have it ___(B)___ .

(A)	(B)
to have this watch repaired	by next week
to get this suit pressed	on Monday evening
to have this package sent to New York	there in time for the holiday
to get this thing changed	early in the week
to have this thing repaired	before Wednesday

Conversation A

S1. How much vacation time do you get?
S2. Only two weeks this year, but three weeks next year.
S1. We get four weeks a year after five years of service.
S2. I may take an extra week without pay this year.

Conversation B

S1. Where do you plan to go for your vacation?
S2. I'm going to Denmark.
S1. When will you be back?
S2. Probably in three or four weeks.

Conversation C

S1. Are you going to take your vacation in June or July?
S2. I'm going to take it in July.
S1. Are you going to go to Europe?
S2. No. I'm going to go to South America.

Conversation D

S1. Did you have a good vacation?
S2. Yes, I did. I had a wonderful time.
S1. What did you do?
S2. I visited some old friends in Florida.

Conversation E

S1. You haven't been around for a long time.
S2. I've been away on a vacation.
S1. Everyone's been asking for you.
S2. It's nice to be missed.

Conversation A

S1. Did you have a nice time over the weekend?
S2. I had lots of fun.
S1. What did you do?
S2. I did a lot of sight-seeing.

Conversation B

S1. How long were you out of town?
S2. I was away for two weeks.
S1. When were you away?
S2. I took the time off in August.

Conversation C

S1. How did you go to India last month?
S2. We went by plane.
S1. What kind of plane did you take?
S2. It was a jet.

Conversation D

S1. Have you ever been to Italy?
S2. No. I've never been there.
S1. Have you ever been to France?
S2. Yes. I was there last summer.

Conversation E

S1. Did your parents stay in Rome for very long?
S2. Yes. They stayed there for two months.
S1. Did they describe their trip to you?
S2. Yes, and they showed us a lot of photographs.

Conversation A

S1. What did you have for breakfast?
S2. I had coffee, toast, and eggs.
S1. How did you have your eggs?
S2. Soft-boiled, as usual.

Conversation B

S1. How about a cup of coffee?
S2. That sounds good.
S1. I always enjoy coffee after work.
S2. I like it best in the morning.

Conversation C

S1. Would you like to have an orange?
S2. Thanks, but I don't think so.
S1. Oranges are good for you.
S2. I know, but I had one about an hour ago.

Conversation D

S1. Where did you have lunch today?
S2. I ate at the cafeteria with John.
S1. Did you have a good lunch?
S1. Yes. I had a hot roast beef sandwich.

Conversation E

S1. There's a cafeteria over there.
S2. Didn't you eat before we left?
S1. Yes, but I'm hungry again.
S2. Well, I'm still digesting my lunch.

Exercise 1 / Line A1 /

What did you have for breakfast?

lunch	What did you have for lunch?
they	What did they have for lunch?
eat	What did they eat for lunch?
dinner	What did they eat for dinner?
she	What did she eat for dinner?

Exercise 2 / Line A3 /

How did you have your eggs?

coffee	How did you have your coffee?
meat	How did you have your meat?
potatoes	How did you have your potatoes?
vegetables	How did you have your vegetables?
salad	How did you have your salad?

Exercise 3 / Lines A3 and A4 /

Did you have your egg soft-boiled?

hard-boiled	Did you have your eggs hard-boiled?
poached	Did you have your eggs poached?
scrambled	Did you have your eggs scrambled?
fried	Did you have your eggs fried?

Exercise 4 / Lines B1 and B3 /

I always enjoy a cup of coffee after work.

tea	I always enjoy a cup of tea after work.
a glass of milk	I always enjoy a glass of milk after work.
wine	I always enjoy a glass of wine after work.
lemonade	I always enjoy a glass of lemonade after work.

Exercise 5 / Lines C1 and C3 /

Would you like to have an orange?	Oranges are good for you.
Would you like to have an apple?	Apples are good for you.
Would you like to have a banana?	Bananas are good for you.
Would you like to have a lemon?	Lemons are good for you.
Would you like to have a tomato?	Tomatoes are good for you.

Conversation A

S1.   I'd like to order breakfast.
S2.   What can I bring you?
S1.   I'd like coffee, scrambled eggs, and bacon.
S2.   I'll bring the coffee first.

Conversation B

S1.   Please give me a ham sandwich.
S2.   Would you like it on rye bread or white?
S1.   Rye bread, please. With mustard.
S2.   Here it is.

Conversation C

S1.   I'd like a piece of pie now and coffee later, please.
S2.   Do you want cream for your coffee?
S1.   Yes. Cream but no sugar.
S2.   I'll bring the pie right away.

Conversation D

S1.   A hamburger and a cup of coffee, please.
S2.   Here you are.
S1.   How much do I owe you?
S2.   Sixty-two cents.

Conversation E

S1.   What did you order?
S2.   I ordered a sandwich and a cup of coffee.
S1.   What kind of sandwich did you order?
S2.   A bacon, lettuce, and tomato sandwich.

Exercise 1 / Line A3 /

I'd like coffee.	I'd like some coffee, please.
I'd like tea.	I'd like some tea, please.
I'd like orange juice.	I'd like some orange juice, please.
I'd like milk.	I'd like some milk, please.
I'd like hot chocolate.	I'd like some hot chocolate, please.

Exercise 2 / Line B2 /

Would you like some coffee?

orange juice	Would you like some orange juice?
care for	Would you care for some orange juice?
tea	Would you care for some tea?
anyone	Would anyone care for some tea?
wine	Would anyone care for some wine?

Exercise 3 / Line B1 /

Please give me a ham sandwich.

cheese	Please give me a cheese sandwich.
ham and cheese	Please give me a ham and cheese sandwich
roast beef	Please give me a roast beef sandwich.
chicken salad	Please give me a chicken salad sandwich.

Exercise 4 / Line C2 /

Do you want cream for your coffee?

sugar	Do you want sugar for your coffee?
tea	Do you want sugar for your tea?
Would you like	Would you like sugar for your tea?
lemon	Would you like lemon for your tea?
Would you prefer	Would you prefer lemon for your tea?

Exercise 5 / Line E1 /

Did you order some food?	Yes, I did. I ordered some food.
Are you ordering some food?	Yes, I am. I'm ordering some food.
Have you ordered some food?	Yes, I have. I've ordered some food.
Are you going to order some food?	Yes, I am. I'm going to order some food.

Conversation A

S1. Could we have a table for four?
S2. There's a nice table right there by the window.
S1. May we also have the menu right away?
S2. I'll get the menu immediately.

Conversation B

S1. Would you care for some roast beef?
S2. No. I'll have sirloin steak.
S1. How do you like your steak?
S2. I'd prefer it medium rare.

Conversation C

S1. Would you like to have soup?
S2. Yes. Creamed onion, please.
S1. Mashed, boiled, or French-fried potatoes?
S2. I'll have the French-fried.

Conversation D

S1. What vegetables would you like with your dinner?
S2. Carrots, please, and corn with cream sauce.
S1. What kind of dressing do you want on your salad—French?
S2. I believe I'll take Russian dressing tonight.

Conversation E

S1. Would you like to order a dessert?
S2. What kinds of pie do you have?
S1. Peach, lemon cream, and apple.
S2. I'd like lemon cream, please.

Exercise 1 / Lines B1 and C1 /

Would you care for some soup?

broth	Would you care for some broth?
consommé	Would you care for some consommé?
potage	Would you care for some potage?
chowder	Would you care for some chowder?

Exercise 2 / Lines C1, C2, E4 /

I'd like creamed onion soup, please.

mushroom	I'd like mushroom soup, please.
vegetable	I'd like vegetable soup, please.
potato	I'd like potato soup, please.
cream of tomato	I'd like cream of tomato soup, please.

Exercise 3 / Lines C3, C4, D4 /

I believe I'll have mashed potatoes.

baked	I believe I'll have baked potatoes.
scalloped	I believe I'll have scalloped potatoes.
French-fried	I believe I'll have French-fried potatoes.
hashed brown	I believe I'll have hashed brown potatoes.
sweet	I believe I'll have sweet potatoes.

Exercise 4 / Lines C4, D4 /

I think I'll have pie for dessert.

cake	I think I'll have cake for dessert.
pudding	I think I'll have pudding for dessert.
cookies	I think I'll have cookies for dessert.
custard	I think I'll have custard for dessert.
ice cream	I think I'll have ice cream for dessert.

Exercise 5 / Line E4 /

I'd like lemon cream pie, please.

apple	I'd like apple pie, please.
peach	I'd like peach pie, please.
blueberry	I'd like blueberry pie, please.
orange meringue	I'd like orange meringue pie, please.
coconut custard	I'd like coconut custard pie, please.

Conversation A

S1. What'll you have, sir?
S2. May I have a menu, please?
S1. A menu? Here you are, sir.
S2. Now, I'll need a few minutes to look it over.

Conversation B

S1. I'll have the sirloin steak listed here.
S2. How do you like your steak—well done?
S1. No. I'd prefer it medium rare.
S2. I'm sure you'll enjoy our steak.

Conversation C

S1. Would you care for soup?
S2. Yes, I would. Vegetable soup, please.
S1. What would you like for your main course?
S2. I'm going to have beef stew for my main course.

Conversation D

S1. Would you care for dessert after your main course?
S2. Possibly. What kind of pie do you have?
S1. Peach, banana cream, and blueberry chiffon.
S2. I think I'd like to try the banana cream.

Conversation E

S1. Coffee, tea, or milk?
S2. Coffee—with the meal, please.
S1. Do you want cream and sugar?
S2. No. I'll take my coffee black.

Exercise 1 / Line B1 /

I'll have the sirloin steak listed here.

pot roast	I'll have the pot roast listed here.
roast beef	I'll have the roast beef listed here.
barbecued beef	I'll have the barbecued beef listed here.
filet mignon	I'll have the filet mignon listed here.
Swiss steak	I'll have the Swiss steak listed here.
lamb curry	I'll have the lamb curry listed here.
breaded veal cutlets	I'll have the breaded veal cutlets listed here.
veal patties	I'll have the veal patties listed here.
veal parmesan	I'll have the veal parmesan listed here.
broiled pork chops	I'll have the broiled pork chops listed here.
stuffed pork chops	I'll have the stuffed pork chops listed here.
baked spareribs	I'll have the baked spareribs listed here.
barbecued spareribs	I'll have the barbecued spareribs listed here.
meat loaf	I'll have the meat loaf listed here.
ham loaf	I'll have the ham loaf listed here.

Exercise 2 / Line C4 /

I'm going to have beef stew.

pork sausages	I'm going to have pork sausages.
browned hash	I'm going to have browned hash.
meat croquettes	I'm going to have meat croquettes.
Swedish meatballs	I'm going to have Swedish meatballs
Hungarian goulash	I'm going to have Hungarian goulash
calf's liver	I'm going to have calf's liver.
broiled duckling	I'm going to have broiled duckling.
fried chicken	I'm going to have fried chicken.
stewed chicken	I'm going to have stewed chicken.
roast turkey	I'm going to have roast turkey.
broiled lobster	I'm going to have broiled lobster.
scalloped oysters	I'm going to have scalloped oysters.
steamed clams	I'm going to have steamed clams.

Conversation A

S1. I hope you're hungry tonight.
S2. I'm sure I'll have a good appetite.
S1. There's a menu right beside you.
S2. Thanks. I see it.

Conversation B

S1. What do you usually have for dinner?
S2. Potatoes and some kind of meat.
S1. Do you ever have anything else?
S2. Oh, I have other things—for example, fish, rice, and vegetables

Conversation C

S1. The fish is delicious in this restaurant, I hear.
S2. It's a popular dish in this country.
S1. But I always choose steak if possible.
S2. Well, I'm going to have fish.

Conversation D

S1. Do you like vegetables?
S2. I like some but not all.
S1. What kind do you like?
S2. I like lettuce and radishes and a few others.

Conversation E

S1. Do you always drink tea with your meals?
S2. Not always, but usually.
S1. How do you like your tea?
S2. With sugar and lemon.

Exercise 1 / Line A1 /

I hope you're hungry tonight.

ready to eat	I hope you're ready to eat tonight.
have a good appetite	I hope you have a good appetite tonight.
feel like eating well	I hope you feel like eating well tonight.
order enough food	I hope you order enough food tonight.
something different	I hope you order something different tonight.

Exercise 2 / Line C1 /

The fish is delicious in this restaurant.

wonderful	The fish is wonderful in this restaurant.
The meat	The meat is wonderful in this restaurant.
always	The meat is always wonderful in this restaurant.
excellent	The meat is always excellent in this restaurant.
The chicken	The chicken is always excellent in this restaurant.

Exercise 3 / Line C2 /

That's a popular dish in this country.

kind of food	That's a popular kind of food in this country.
famous	That's a famous kind of food in this country.
the United States	That's a famous kind of food in the United States.
kind of meal	That's a famous kind of meal in the United States.
well-known	That's a well-known kind of meal in the United States.

Exercise 4 / Line E1 /

Do you always drink tea with your meals?

coffee	Do you always drink coffee with your meals?
usually	Do you usually drink coffee with your meals?
at breakfast	Do you usually drink coffee at breakfast?
milk	Do you usually drink milk at breakfast?
generally	Do you generally drink milk at breakfast?

Conversation A

S1. You look very pale.
S2. I feel rather dizzy, and I have a headache.
S1. Maybe you're catching a cold.
S2. You're probably right.

Conversation B

S1. You went to the doctor today, didn't you?
S2. Yes. I go once a year for a checkup.
S1. What did he say?
S2. He said my health was good.

Conversation C

S1. Have you put on weight recently?
S2. I probably have.
S1. Maybe you don't get enough exercise.
S2. I really don't, but I'm careful about eating.

Conversation D

S1. You certainly look very healthy to me.
S2. I've been feeling very well lately.
S1. Haven't you gotten a little heavier?
S2. Yes, I think I have.

Conversation E

S1. You certainly look happy about something.
S2. I've lost some weight.
S1. You look much better.
S2. I feel better too.

Exercise 1 / Line A1 /

You look very pale.

rested	You look very rested.
sunburned	You look very sunburned.
healthy	You look very healthy.
well	You look very well.
sleepy	You look very sleepy.

Exercise 2 / Line E1 /

You certainly look happy about something.

angry	You certainly look angry about something.
excited	You certainly look excited about something.
nervous	You certainly look nervous about something.
upset	You certainly look upset about something.

Exercise 3 / Line A2 /

I feel rather dizzy.

feverish	I feel rather feverish.
quite	I feel quite feverish.
nauseous	I feel quite nauseous.
a little	I feel a little nauseous.
sick to my stomach	I feel a little sick to my stomach.

Exercise 4 / Line B2 /

I go once a year for a checkup.

twice	I go twice a year for a checkup.
several times a year	I go several times a year for a checkup.
every other year	I go every other year for a checkup.
every two years	I go every two years for a checkup.

Exercise 5 / Line C1 /

Have you put on weight recently?

Mary	Has Mary put on weight recently?
lost weight	Has Mary lost weight recently?
your friends	Have your friends lost weight recently?
been on a diet	Have your friends been on a diet recently?
Mrs. Brown	Has Mrs. Brown been on a diet recently?

Conversation A

S1. I have a terrible headache today.
S2. Have you taken any aspirin for it?
S1. Yes. I'll get over it soon.
S2. Lying down for a few minutes might help it too.

Conversation B

S1. I've got a cold in my head.
S2. It's probably this terrible weather.
S1. Yes. It's giving everyone a cold.
S2. I hope I don't catch one.

Conversation C

S1. What are you taking for your cold?
S2. Just the usual things—water and fruit juice.
S1. You'll be over it soon then.
S2. I really hope you're right.

Conversation D

S1. You look tired. Are you ill?
S2. I think I've caught a cold.
S1. How can you tell?
S2. My throat is sore.

Conversation E

S1. You don't look very well.
S2. I don't feel very well either.
S1. Why don't you rest for a few minutes?
S2. I think I will.

Exercise 1 / Line A1 /

I have a terrible headache today.

stomachache	I have a terrible stomachache today.
severe	I have a severe stomachache today.
backache	I have a severe backache today.
very bad	I have a very bad backache today.
earache	I have a very bad earache today.

Exercise 2 / Line A4 /

Lying down might help it too.

taking some medicine	Taking some medicine might help it too.
resting a while	Resting a while might help it too.
going to bed	Going to bed might help it too.
drinking some tea	Drinking some tea might help it too.

Exercise 3 / Line C1 /

What are you doing for your cold?

toothache	What are you doing for your toothache?
upset stomach	What are you doing for your upset stomach?
rheumatism	What are you doing for your rheumatism?
sore throat	What are you doing for your sore throat?

Exercise 4 / Line D2 /

I think I've caught a cold.

broken my finger	I think I've broken my finger.
scratched my arm	I think I've scratched my arm.
injured my knee	I think I've injured my knee.
hurt my shoulder	I think I've hurt my shoulder.

Exercise 5 / Line D4 /

My throat is sore.

toes	My toes are sore.
leg	My leg is sore.
shoulders	My shoulders are sore.
wrist	My wrist is sore.
chest	My chest is sore.

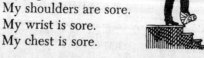

Conversation A

S1. I think I've got a fever.
S2. Do you feel very hot?
S1. Yes, and I've been sweating a lot.
S2. You'd better go to a doctor.

Conversation B

S1. I feel quite sick, Doctor.
S2. Can you tell me about it?
S1. I've got a headache and stomach cramps.
S2. I'd better take your temperature.

Conversation C

S1. Is the cut on my hand dangerous?
S2. No, but there's a little infection.
S1. What can you do about an infection?
S2. I'll use an antibiotic, and it'll be gone by tomorrow.

Conversation D

S1. Have you ever had pneumonia?
S2. Yes. I had it about two years ago.
S1. Have you ever had measles?
S2. No. I've never had measles.

Conversation E

S1. Do I have anything serious, Doctor?
S2. Only a slight cold.
S1. Will it last very long?
S2. No. It'll probably go away in a day or two.

Exercise 1 / Line A1 /

I think I've got a fever.

a rash	I think I've got a rash.
an allergy	I think I've got an allergy.
an infection	I think I've got an infection.
a blister	I think I've got a blister.
an inflammation	I think I've got an inflammation.
an abscess	I think I've got an abscess.

Exercise 2 / Line C3 /

What can you do about an infection?

appendicitis	What can you do about appendicitis?
flu	What can you do about flu?
an abscess	What can you do about an abscess?
diarrhea	What can you do about diarrhea?
insomnia	What can you do about insomnia?
a sore throat	What can you do about a sore throat?

Exercise 3 / Line D1 /

Have you ever had pneumonia?

hay fever	Have you ever had hay fever?
asthma	Have you ever had asthma?
rheumatism	Have you ever had rheumatism?
sinus trouble	Have you ever had sinus trouble?
ulcers	Have you ever had ulcers?
low blood pressure	Have you ever had low blood pressure?

Exercise 4 / Line D4 /

I've never had measles.

mumps	I've never had mumps.
scarlet fever	I've never had scarlet fever.
chicken pox	I've never had chicken pox.
smallpox	I've never had smallpox.
tuberculosis	I've never had tuberculosis.
malaria	I've never had malaria.

Exercise 5 / Line E4

It'll probably go away in a day or two.

an hour or two from now	It'll probably go away an hour or two from now.
in a matter of minutes	It'll probably go away in a matter of minutes.
in a short time	It'll probably go away in a short time.
within a few hours	It'll probably go away within a few hours.
before you get home	It'll probably go away before you get home.

Conversation A

S1.   How did you find your new job?
S2.   I went to an employment agency.
S1.   Was it worth it to do it that way?
S2.   Yes. They were able to get me something good right away.

Conversation B

S1.   I think I'm going to change jobs.
S2.   What do you want to do that for?
S1.   There's not enough chance to get ahead here.
S2.   But don't forget you're getting a pretty good salary.

Conversation C

S1.   Did it take you long to apply for a job?
S2.   Too long in my opinion.
S1.   What did you have to do?
S2.   Speak to people, fill out forms, and wait.

Conversation D

S1.   Is John going to quit his job next month?
S2.   No. He's going to quit next January.
S1.   Are his parents going to support him then?
S2.   No. He isn't going to ask them for any money.

Conversation E

S1.   I'd like to speak to the personnel manager, please.
S2.   May I ask what it's about?
S1.   I'd like to see him about the position advertised in today's
      newspaper.
S2.   Certainly. Just have a seat over there for a moment.

Conversation A

S1. How long has that man been over there at the desk?
S2. About a minute or two, I think.
S1. Can you find out what he wants?
S2. I'll ask him right away.

Conversation B

S1. Has the secretary sent the letter yet?
S2. Yes. She's already sent them the letter.
S1. She still hasn't sent a copy of the letter to me.
S2. I forgot to tell you she gave me your copy.

Conversation C

S1. To whom did you send the invoice?
S2. I sent it to the General Sales Company.
S1. Specifically, whom did you address it to?
S2. I addressed it to the purchasing agent.

Conversation D

S1. Have you finished the report on current inventory yet?
S2. No, I haven't, but I certainly wish I had.
S1. Why haven't you finished it?
S2. I didn't have enough time to spend on it yesterday.

Conversation E

S1. I'm having some trouble with this sales-volume report.
S2. You didn't have any trouble with your report last week.
S1. Well, there are some difficult parts in this one.
S2. I'm sorry, but I don't have any suggestions.

Conversation A

S1. What did you spend all your time on today?
S2. Checking the annual report.
S1. Was everything in it all right?
S2. No. I discovered several errors.

Conversation B

S1. How is the mail handled?
S2. The executive secretary opens it and sorts it out.
S1. Is any record kept of incoming mail?
S2. Yes. Everything is entered on the mail register.

Conversation C

S1. Do you receive many inquiries about your product?
S2. Yes. There are a good number every day.
S1. You can't answer all of them personally, can you?
S2. No. Unless they're obviously important, we send back a form letter.

Conversation D

S1. I'd like to dictate a letter to the A.B.C. Company.
S2. Just a moment please, while I get my shorthand notebook.
S1. Would you also bring me the previous correspondence with them?
S2. I've already put the file on your desk.

Conversation E

S1. I've been working very hard recently.
S2. How come you've been working so hard?
S1. I've been trying to impress my boss.
S2. I hope you haven't been working in vain.

Conversation A

S1. Does Dr. Taylor teach every day?
S2. No. Only Monday, Wednesday, and Friday.
S1. Is Dr. Taylor teaching right now?
S2. No, he isn't. He's working in his office.

Conversation B

S1. Why doesn't John practice anymore?
S2. He doesn't have much free time.
S1. He used to have a lot of free time, didn't he?
S2. Yes, he did, but now he's going to school every night.

Conversation C

S1. What are you studying this semester?
S2. History, English, and math.
S1. Which do you like best?
S2. History really interests me the most.

Conversation D

S1. Not all students do their lessons carefully.
S2. Well, I do mine carefully.
S1. But your brother often does his at the last moment.
S2. And my sister always does hers a day or two late.

Conversation E

S1. How come you aren't at school today?
S2. There aren't any classes this week.
S1. Well, how come there aren't any classes?
S2. This is our spring vacation.

Exercise 1 / Lines A1 and A2 /

Does Dr. Taylor teach every day?	He teaches on Monday.
Does Dr. Taylor write every day?	He writes on Tuesday.
Does Dr. Taylor drive every day?	He drives on Wednesday.
Does Dr. Taylor watch every day?	He watches on Thursday.
Does Dr. Taylor listen every day?	He listens on Friday.
Does Dr. Taylor practice every day?	He practices on Saturday.
Does Dr. Taylor rest every day?	He rests on Sunday.

Exercise 2 / Lines A1 and A3 /

Does he teach every day?	Is he teaching right now?
Do they study every day?	Are they studying right now?
Do you practice every day?	Are you practicing right now?
Does she drive every day?	Is she driving right now?
Do they watch every day?	Are they watching right now?
Does he listen every day?	Is he listening right now?
Do you rest every day?	Are you resting right now?

Exercise 3 / Lines A1 and A3 /

They listen every day.	Do they listen every day?
He's studying right now.	Is he studying right now?
She walks every day.	Does she walk every day?
I'm practicing right now.	Are you practicing right now?
They drive every day.	Do they drive every day?
He's teaching right now.	Is he teaching right now?

Exercise 4 / Line B1 /

John doesn't practice anymore.	Why doesn't John practice anymore?
We don't practice anymore.	Why don't you practice anymore?
They don't practice anymore.	Why don't they practice anymore?
Mary doesn't practice anymore.	Why doesn't Mary practice anymore?
I don't practice anymore.	Why don't you practice anymore?
The boys don't practice anymore.	Why don't the boys practice anymore?

Exercise 5 / Line B2 /

He doesn't have much time.	He has a lot of time.
He doesn't have many friends.	He has a lot of friends.
He doesn't have much experience.	He has a lot of experience.
He doesn't have many books.	He has a lot of books.
He doesn't have much information.	He has a lot of information.
He doesn't have much training.	He has a lot of training.
He doesn't have much money.	He has a lot of money.

Exercise 6 / Line B3 /

He had a lot of time.	He had lots of time.
He had a lot of friends.	He had lots of friends.
He had a lot of experience.	He had lots of experience.
He had a lot of books.	He had lots of books.
He had a lot of information.	He had lots of information.
He had a lot of training.	He had lots of training.
He had a lot of money.	He had lots of money.

Exercise 7 / Line B3 /

He used to have a lot of free time.

practice every day	He used to practice every day.
study almost every night	He used to study almost every night.
read a lot of books	He used to read a lot of books.
learn everything by heart	He used to learn everything by heart.
be a good student	He used to be a good student.

Exercise 8 / Line B3 /

He used to have a lot of free time.	But he doesn't any more.
They used to practice every day.	But they don't any more.
She used to study almost every night.	But she doesn't any more.
I used to read a lot of books.	But I don't any more.
You used to learn everything by heart.	But you don't any more.
He used to work in the evening.	But he doesn't any more.

Exercise 9 / Line B4 /

He's going to school every night.

We	We're going to school every night.
They	They're going to school every night.
I	I'm going to school every night.
She	She's going to school every night.
Tom and I	Tom and I are going to school every night.

Exercise 10 / Line C1 /

I'm studying English this semester.

What are you studying this semester?

She's studying geography this semester.

What's she studying this semester?

They're studying history this semester.

What are they studying this semester?

We're studying math this semester.

What are you studying this semester?

He's studying chemistry this semester.

What's he studying this semester?

Tom and I are studying physics this semester.

What are Tom and you studying this semester?

Exercise 11 / Line C4 /

History really interests me the most.

Chemistry	Chemistry really interests me the most.
English	English really interests me the most.
Math	Math really interests me the most.
Geography	Geography really interests me the most.
Physics	Physics really interests me the most.

Exercise 12 / Line D1 /

Not all students do their lessons carefully.

correctly	Not all students do their lessons correctly.
practice	Not all students practice their lessons correctly.
thoroughly	Not all students practice their lessons thoroughly.
go over	Not all students go over their lessons thoroughly.
promptly	Not all students go over their lessons promptly.

Exercise 13 / Line E1 /

How come you aren't at school today?	Why aren't you at school today?
How come he isn't at school today?	Why isn't he at school today?
How come they aren't at school today?	Why aren't they at school today?
How come she isn't at school today?	Why isn't she at school today?
How come Tom and you aren't at school today?	Why aren't Tom and you at school today?
How come the girls aren't at school today?	Why aren't the girls at school today?

Exercise 14 / Line E2 /

There aren't any classes this week.

meetings	There aren't any meetings this week.
lectures	There aren't any lectures this week.
concerts	There aren't any concerts this week.
discussions	There aren't any discussions this week.
examinations	There aren't any examinations this week.

Exercise 15 / Line E2 /

There aren't any classes this week.

meetings	There aren't any meetings this week.
today or tomorrow	There aren't any meetings today or tomorrow.
lectures	There aren't any lectures today or tomorrow.
during our vacation	There aren't any lectures during our vacation.
examinations	There aren't any examinations during our vacation.

Conversation A

S1.   Why are you so worried?
S2.   My sister doesn't study hard enough.
S1.   Isn't she interested in school?
S2.   School interests her, but homework doesn't.

Conversation B

S1.   I'm worried about my school work.
S2.   What's the problem?
S1.   I think I'm going to fail the examinations.
S2.   Maybe you won't if you have more confidence.

Conversation C

S1.   What are you going to study at the University?
S2.   Probably history and English.
S1.   You'll have to work hard.
S2.   Yes. I've heard that it's a difficult school.

Conversation D

S1.   What did you apply for?
S2.   I applied for a scholarship.
S1.   What school did you apply to?
S2.   I applied to Eastern State College.

Conversation E

S1.   I understand the boys' applications were turned down.
S2   Who turned them down?
S1.   I think the college admissions committee.
S2.   I'd advise them to try again.

Exercise 1 / Line A2 /

My sister doesn't study hard enough.

carefully	My sister doesn't study carefully enough.
read	My sister doesn't read carefully enough.
thoroughly	My sister doesn't read thoroughly enough.
practice	My sister doesn't practice thoroughly enough.
long enough	My sister doesn't practice long enough.

Exercise 2 / Line A3 /

Isn't she interested in that?	She's interested in that, isn't she?
Isn't she satisfied with that?	She's satisfied with that, isn't she?
Isn't she annoyed over that?	She's annoyed over that, isn't she?
Isn't she accustomed to that?	She's accustomed to that, isn't she?
Isn't she adjusted to that?	She's adjusted to that, isn't she?
Isn't she concerned about that?	She's concerned about that, isn't she?

Exercise 3 / Line A3 /

Isn't she interested in school?

tired of	Isn't she tired of school?
her work	Isn't she tired of her work?
satisfied with	Isn't she satisfied with her work?
annoyed over	Isn't she annoyed over her work?
all the changes	Isn't she annoyed over all the changes?
accustomed to	Isn't she accustomed to all the changes?
worried about	Isn't she worried about all the changes?
getting a job	Isn't she worried about getting a job?
concerned about	Isn't she concerned about getting a job?
excited about	Isn't she excited about getting a job?
studying English	Isn't she excited about studying English?
involved in	Isn't she involved in studying English?
adjusted to	Isn't she adjusted to studying English?
our new schedule	Isn't she adjusted to our new schedule?
disappointed in	Isn't she disappointed in our new schedule?

Exercise 4 / Line D1 /

What did you apply for?

complain about	What did you complain about?
comment on	What did you comment on?
listen to	What did you listen to?
succeed in	What did you succeed in?

Exercise 5 / Line D1 /

Did you apply for a scholarship? — What did you apply for?

Did you complain about the noise? — What did you complain about?

Did you comment on the suggestion? — What did you comment on?

Did you listen to that program? — What did you listen to?

Did you succeed in your work? — What did you succeed in?

Exercise 6 / Lines E1 and E2 /

They were turned down. — Who turned them down?

They were looked over. — Who looked them over?

They were thrown away. — Who threw them away?

They were taken back. — Who took them back?

They were used up. — Who used them up?

They were given away. — Who gave them away?

Exercise 7 / Line E4 /

I'd advise them to try again.

ask	I'd ask them to try again.
urge	I'd urge them to try again.
force	I'd force them to try again.
instruct	I'd instruct them to try again.
persuade	I'd persuade them to try again.

Exercise 8 / Line E4 /

They advised him to go. — He was advised to go.

They asked him to go. — He was asked to go.

They urged him to go. — He was urged to go.

They forced him to go. — He was forced to go.

They instructed him to go. — He was instructed to go.

They persuaded him to go. — He was persuaded to go.

Conversation A

S1.   English is the hardest language in the world.
S2.   Why do you say that?
S1.   I can't understand it or speak it.
S2.   But this is only your first day in the English class!

Conversation B

S1.   How do you pronounce this word in English?
S2.   It's pronounced "sign."
S1.   What's a "sign"?
S2.   It's a "public notice."

Conversation C

S1.   What do you call this thing in English?
S2.   It's a "hammer."
S1.   What's the word for the things you hit with a hammer?
S2.   "Nails." You pound nails into wood with a hammer.

Conversation D

S1.   How do you ask for help politely?
S2.   You say, "Could you help me, please?"
S1.   Is it all right to say, "Could you please help me?"
S2.   Yes. You can say it that way too.

Conversation E

S1.   Can you understand spoken English very well?
S2.   I can understand you, but most people speak too fast.
S1.   How about speaking? Can you carry on a conversation?
S2.   I'm really not very fluent yet.

Exercise 1 / Line A1 /

English is hard.	It's the hardest language in the world.
English is difficult.	It's the most difficult language in the world.
English is easy.	It's the easiest language in the world.
English is complicated.	It's the most complicated language in the world.
English is simple.	It's the simplest language in the world.

Exercise 2 / Line A4 /

This is your first day in the class.

week	This is your first week in the class.
the office	This is your first week in the office.
third	This is your third week in the office.
month	This is your third month in the office.
factory	This is your third month in the factory.

Exercise 3 / Lines D2 and D3 /

Could you help me, please?	Could you please help me?
Could you come here, please?	Could you please come here?
Could you wait there, please?	Could you please wait there?
Could you correct this, please?	Could you please correct this?
Could you translate it, please?	Could you please translate it?

Exercise 4 / Line D3 /

Is it all right to say that?

correct	Is it correct to say that?
incorrect	Is it incorrect to say that?
proper	Is it proper to say that?
improper	Is it improper to say that?
polite	Is it polite to say that?
impolite	Is it impolite to say that?

Exercise 5 / Line E3 /

Can you speak?	How about speaking?
Can you write?	How about writing?
Can you read?	How about reading?
Can you follow it?	How about following it?
Can you pronounce it?	How about pronouncing it?

Conversation A

S1. Do you want to learn English?
S2. Yes, I do—very much.
S1. Why do you want to learn English?
S2. Because it'll be useful in the future.

Conversation B

S1. I want to learn English.
S2. Then you must speak it.
S1. Why must I speak it?
S2. Because you want to learn it.

Conversation C

S1. Do you understand the sentence?
S2. I don't understand it completely.
S1. All right, then. I'll repeat it.
S2. Thank you very much.

Conversation D

S1. Did you understand what I said?
S2. No, I didn't. Would you please say it again?
S1. Of course. I'll say it again slowly.
S2. That will help a lot.

Conversation E

S1. Please write down John's address.
S2. All right, but would you please speak very slowly?
S1. Yes. Do you want me to spell each word too?
S2. Not the numbers—only the names.

Conversation A

S1.   What are you studying right now?
S2.   I'm doing my English assignment.
S1.   What's the hardest thing about English?
S2.   Pronunciation is the hardest thing for me.

Conversation B

S1.   Can Peter understand French as well as English?
S2.   Yes, and he can speak it well too.
S1.   I can't speak a word of any language except my own.
S2.   Neither can I.

Conversation C

S1.   That man is able to speak three or four languages.
S2.   Yes, and he can speak them well, I understand.
S1.   Could you learn three or four languages?
S2.   I could if I had a hundred years to do it.

Conversation D

S1.   I'm feeling very discouraged.
S2.   What's the matter?
S1.   When people talk to me, they talk too fast.
S2.   You'll have to listen faster then.

Conversation E

S1.   Learning languages is difficult.
S2   I wish there were only one language in the world.
S1.   Then we'd have to learn it.
S2.   That's the trouble, isn't it?

Conversation A

S1. Why don't we park the car there?
S2. That's a no-parking zone.
S1. There are parking meters in the next block.
S2. Let's see if we can find a space there then.

Conversation B

S1. You'd better turn left at the next corner.
S2. I can't—no left turn.
S1. Then we'll have to drive around the block.
S2. It looks like it.

Conversation C

S1. You're driving too fast.
S2. What's the speed limit?
S1. It's fifty miles per hour.
S2. Then, I'm under the limit.

Conversation D

S1. How do you like your new car?
S2. Great! I really like the automatic shift.
S1. Does it have power steering?
S2. Yes, and it's got power brakes too.

Conversation E

S1. You drive very well.
S2. Thanks. I always try to be cautious.
S1. You are, but best of all, you drive very smoothly.
S2. Steady pressure on the accelerator and brakes is important

Conversation A

S1. My car won't start.
S2. Press the starter button.
S1. Nothing happens when I press the starter.
S2. Then your battery is dead.

Conversation B

S1. Could you help me for a moment, please?
S2. What can I do for you?
S1. Could you look over my radiator?
S2. I'll check it after I help that other man.

Conversation C

S1. What's your brother doing?
S2. He's fixing the motor of the car.
S1. Does he need any help?
S2. I don't think so.

Conversation D

S1. Could you look over my car?
S2. What's the matter?
S1. Well, I don't know.
S2. I can look at it now if you can wait.

Conversation E

S1. Could you change my right tire, please? It's flat.
S2. Certainly. Do you want us to fix it too?
S1. Would you please?
S2. We'll have it ready for you tomorrow morning.

Conversation A

S1. Where were you born?
S2. I was born here.
S1. Have you lived here all your life?
S2. Yes, I have.

Conversation B

S1. Whom will you get the money from?
S2. We'll get it from our parents.
S1. What will you spend the money on?
S2. We'll spend it on books and supplies.

Conversation C

S1. Do you want me to wait for you?
S2. No. I can take care of everything myself.
S1. Can't we get together a little later then?
S2. Sure. I'll be through in about half an hour.

Conversation D

S1. What took you so long?
S2. I had a lot of things to do.
S1. We'd better hurry, or we'll be late.
S2. I think you're right.

Conversation E

S1. I'm starting my vacation next week.
S2. You ought to see as much as you can.
S1. That's what I think too.
S2. You really ought to travel by bus then.

83. General Conversations (2)

Conversation A

S1. Where did you get that book?
S2. From the library in my neighborhood.
S1. Is it a good library?
S2. Come with me and see for yourself.

Conversation B

S1. We're going to be late for the meeting.
S2. When does it start?
S1. It starts in exactly fifteen minutes.
S2. I think we'll be on time.

Conversation C

S1. Something is bothering me.
S2. What's bothering you?
S1. I think I left the lights on in my apartment.
S2. Well, there's nothing you can do about it now.

Conversation D

S1. What does that sign say?
S2. It says "No Smoking."
S1. What are you doing?
S2. I'm putting out my cigarette.

Conversation E

S1. I'm sorry I'm late for our appointment.
S2. What happened?
S1. The traffic was very heavy.
S2. It's always bad at this time of the day.

Conversation A

S1.   Where's Mrs. King?
S2.   She's in the other office right now.
S1.   Do you expect her back soon?
S2.   Yes, I do. In just a few minutes.

Conversation B

S1.   Someone wants to talk to you on the telephone.
S2.   Who is it? Do you know?
S1.   I'm sorry, but I forgot to ask.
S2.   It's OK. I think I know who it is.

Conversation C

S1.   Will there be a meeting here next week?
S2.   No, but there'll be one on the twentieth.
S1.   Will there be many people at the meeting?
S2.   According to John, there will.

Conversation D

S1.   Why do you have to go to Hawaii?
S2.   I'm going for business reasons.
S1.   How will you travel, by boat or by plane?
S2.   Most likely, I'll go by plane.

Conversation E

S1.   Would you like to go to the store with us?
S2.   I'd like to, but I've got to do some work.
S1.   Why don't you do it later?
S2.   I wish I could, but I can't.

Conversation A

S1. Would you like to see some pictures?
S2. Sure. Did you take them yourself?
S1. Yes, I did. I've got a new camera.
S2. These are really wonderful!

Conversation B

S1. I've got to visit my mother tonight.
S2. Is she expecting you?
S1. Yes, she is. I phoned her this morning.
S2. Have a nice time, then.

Conversation C

S1. Could I speak to your brother, please?
S2. Sorry. He isn't here right now.
S1. What time do you expect him back?
S2. About five or five thirty.

Conversation D

S1. Why doesn't Harry go to school here anymore?
S2. His family moved away.
S1. Is he going to another school now?
S2. Yes. Somewhere on the West Coast.

Conversation E

S1. How do you operate this machine?
S2. You turn the lever to the right.
S1. Do you turn it all the way to the right?
S2. No. You turn it to the first mark.

Conversation A

S1. I'd like to speak to Mr. Smith.
S2. Sorry. He isn't in now.
S1. Can I leave a message for him?
S2. Yes. I'll take the message.

Conversation B

S1. Fred has to stay home, but I don't.
S2. I don't either.
S1. Would you like to go with John and me?
S2. Yes, I certainly would.

Conversation C

S1. Where were you last Tuesday and Wednesday?
S2. I was out of town.
S1. Why did you leave town so suddenly?
S2. A friend was sick and needed help.

Conversation D

S1. That's a good-looking suit you have on.
S2. Thank you for the compliment.
S1. When did you get it?
S2. About two or three weeks ago.

Conversation E

S1. John hasn't called us yet.
S2. I thought he called you yesterday.
S1. No. We didn't hear from him at all.
S2. I wonder what happened?

Conversation A

S1. What's the matter?
S2. I'm worried about something.
S1. What's wrong?
S2. I think I've lost my billfold.

Conversation B

S1. Are you coming to the meeting tomorrow?
S2. Of course I'm coming.
S1. Aren't you worried about driving in this weather?
S2. Of course not.

Conversation C

S1. How do you start this machine?
S2. You just push the red button.
S1. Where's the button?
S2. It's right in front of you.

Conversation D

S1. Well, it's cool and cloudy again today.
S2. I wish that the sun were out.
S1. It looks to me as if it's going to rain.
S2. The farmers would like it if it did.

Conversation E

S1. If you had a lot of money, what would you buy?
S2. I think I'd buy a big boat.
S1. What would you do with it?
S2. I'd take all my friends around the world.

Part 2:

Structural Conversations

Conversation A

S1.   Fred practices very hard, I notice.
S2.   Does he practice every day?
S1.   Yes, he does.
S2.   I don't practice that much.

Conversation B

S1.   I'm having some trouble with my report.
S2.   Are you having trouble with the last part?
S1.   Yes, I am.
S2.   Well, everyone is having trouble with that part.

Conversation C

S1.   We saw the new flower show.
S2.   Did you see it on the opening day?
S1.   Yes, we did.
S2.   We didn't see it until the following day.

Conversation D

S1.   Did you write letters to all your friends?
S2.   No, but I wrote letters to some of them.
S1.   Are you going to write to everyone?
S2.   Well, I'm going to write to as many as possible.

Conversation E

S1.   Mary has only worn her new coat twice.
S2.   Has she worn her new spring suit yet?
S1.   Yes, she has. Several times, in fact.
S2.   I know she hasn't worn her new shoes yet.

Exercise 1

1. John studies.
   every day
   (?)

   Does John study?
   Does John study every day?
   Yes, he does. He studies every day.

2. Fred doesn't study.
   every day
   (?)

   Doesn't Fred study?
   Doesn't Fred study every day?
   No, he doesn't. He doesn't study every day.

3. The girl is studying.
   right now
   (?)

   Is the girl studying?
   Is the girl studying right now?
   Yes, she is. She's studying right now.

4. They aren't studying.
   right now
   (?)

   Aren't they studying?
   Aren't they studying right now?
   No, they aren't. They aren't studying right now.

5. Mary studied.
   yesterday
   (?)

   Did Mary study?
   Did Mary study yesterday?
   Yes, she did. She studied yesterday.

6. Fred didn't study.
   yesterday
   (?)

   Didn't Fred study?
   Didn't Fred study yesterday?
   No, he didn't. He didn't study yesterday.

   I'm going to study.
   tomorrow
   (?)

   Are you going to study?
   Are you going to study tomorrow?
   Yes, I am. I'm going to study tomorrow.

8. He isn't going to study.
   tomorrow
   (?)

   Isn't he going to study?
   Isn't he going to study tomorrow?
   No, he isn't. He isn't going to study tomorrow.

9. The girl will study.
   tomorrow
   (?)

   Will the girl study?
   Will the girl study tomorrow?
   Yes, she will. She'll study tomorrow.

10. The men won't study.   Won't the men study?
     tomorrow   Won't the men study tomorrow?
     (?)   No, they won't. They won't study
                                    tomorrow.

11. John has studied.   Has John studied?
     since June   Has John studied since June?
     (?)   Yes, he has. He's studied since
                                    June.

12. Fred hasn't studied.   Hasn't Fred studied?
     since June   Hasn't Fred studied since June?
     (?)   No, he hasn't. He hasn't studied
                                    since June.

Exercise 2

1. He isn't in his office now.   Isn't he in his office now?
    (?)   No, he isn't. He isn't in his
                                    office now.

2. He works very efficiently.   Does he work very efficiently?
    (?)   Yes, he does. He works very
                                    efficiently.

3. He hasn't tried that   Hasn't he tried that method?
    method.   No, he hasn't. He hasn't tried
    (?)   that method.

4. He wore a new suit yes-   Did he wear a new suit yester-
    terday.   day?
    (?)   Yes, he did. He wore a new suit
                                    yesterday.

5. He couldn't be with them.   Couldn't he be with them?
    (?)   No, he couldn't. He couldn'.
                                    be with them.

6. He won't have enough   Won't he have enough time?
    time.   No, he won't. He won't have
    (?)   enough time.

7. He found the correct an-   Did he find the correct answer?
    swer.   Yes, he did. He found the cor-
    (?)   rect answer.

8. He's forgotten their names. (?)

Has he forgotten their names?
Yes, he has. He's forgotten their names.

9. He wasn't working on that. (?)

Wasn't he working on that?
No, he wasn't. He wasn't working on that.

10. He must rely on his friends. (?)

Must he rely on his friends?
Yes, he must. He must rely on his friends.

11. He has to explain everything. (?)

Does he have to explain everything?
Yes, he does. He has to explain everything.

12. He didn't drive to work today. (?)

Didn't he drive to work today?
No, he didn't. He didn't drive to work today.

13. He shouldn't have waited. (?)

Shouldn't he have waited?
No, he shouldn't have. He shouldn't have waited.

14. He does all his work promptly. (?)

Does he do all his work promptly?
Yes, he does. He does all his work promptly.

15. He'll meet the men there. (?)

Will he meet the men there?
Yes, he will. He'll meet the men there.

16. He used to enjoy baseball. (?)

Did he use to enjoy baseball?
Yes, he did. He used to enjoy baseball.

Conversation A

S1. Don't you work every Saturday morning?
S2. No, we don't. Just on occasion.
S1. Did you work last Saturday morning?
S2. No, we didn't.

Conversation B

S1. Didn't those tourists go to the park yesterday?
S2. Yes, they did.
S1. Did they go with you and John?
S2. No, they didn't, but we saw them there.

Conversation C

S1. Are you going to your class now?
S2. No, I'm not, but I'll be leaving shortly.
S1. Do you go to school every afternoon?
S2. No, I don't. Only Tuesday and Thursday afternoons.

Conversation D

S1. Have you ever been to the Central Zoo?
S2. No, I never have.
S1. Would you care to go there with me tomorrow?
S2. Yes, I certainly would.

Conversation E

S1. Shouldn't you answer their letter quite soon?
S2. Yes, I really should.
S1. Don't you have to send them some money too?
S2. No, I don't. Not in this next letter.

Exercise 1

1.	Are they studying?	Yes, they are.
2.	Won't she study?	Yes, she will.
3.	Did you study?	Yes, I did.
4.	Isn't he studying?	Yes, he is.
5.	Have they studied?	Yes, they have.
6.	Aren't you going to study?	Yes, I am.
7.	Can she study?	Yes, she can.
8.	Doesn't he study?	Yes, he does.
9.	Must they study?	Yes, they must.
10.	Shouldn't you study?	Yes, I should.
11.	Couldn't she study?	Yes, she could.
12.	Did he use to study?	Yes, he did.
13.	Aren't they supposed to study?	Yes, they are.
14.	Will she study?	Yes, she will.
15.	Hadn't you better study?	Yes, I'd better.
16.	Do they have to study?	Yes, they do.
17.	Don't they plan to study?	Yes, they do.
18.	Were they studying?	Yes, they were.

Exercise 2

1.	Shouldn't they do it?	No, they shouldn't.
2.	Does he do it?	No, he doesn't.
3.	Can't you do it?	No, I can't.
4.	Are they going to do it?	No, they aren't.
5.	Hasn't she done it?	No, she hasn't.
6.	Did he do it?	No, he didn't.
7.	Won't you do it?	No, I won't.
8.	Isn't she doing it?	No, she isn't.
9.	Do they have to do it?	No, they don't.
10.	Hadn't you better do it?	No, I hadn't better.
11.	Did she use to do it?	No, she didn't.
12.	Couldn't they do it?	No, they couldn't.
13.	Must he do it?	No, he doesn't have to
14.	Weren't you supposed to do it?	No, I wasn't.
15.	Has he done it?	No, he hasn't.
16.	Did they use to do it?	No, they didn't.
17.	Wasn't she doing it?	No, she wasn't.
18.	Has he been doing it?	No, he hasn't.

Conversation A

S1. Are you going to attend the reception?
S2. Yes, I am.
S1. Are you going to stay very late?
S2. No, I'm not.

Conversation B

S1. Are there many rooms in their apartment?
S2. Yes, there are. About six, I think.
S1. Is there much light in the apartment?
S2. No, there isn't, because there are very few windows.

Conversation C

S1. Are you reading that magazine?
S2. Yes, I am. I'm reading the book review.
S1. Are you using your dictionary?
S2. No, I'm not, but I'm doing quite well.

Conversation D

S1. Has John spoken to you yet?
S2. Yes, he has, and he's spoken to Mrs. White too.
S1. Did he speak to you yesterday?
S2. Yes, he did. Around four o'clock.

Conversation E

S1. Will Mary be at the party?
S2. Yes, she will, but she'll be a little late.
S1. Will she be with her weekend guests?
S2. No, she won't.

Exercise 1

1.	Does he practice?	Yes, he does.
2.	Will he practice?	Yes, he will.
3.	Can he practice?	Yes, he can.
4.	What does he do?	He practices.
5.	What'll he do?	He'll practice.
6.	What can he do?	He can practice.
7.	Should they read?	Yes, they should.
8.	Have they read?	Yes, they have.
9.	Are they reading?	Yes, they are.
10.	What should they do?	They should read.
11.	What have they done?	They've read.
12.	What are they doing?	They're reading.
13.	Did you copy them?	Yes, I did.
14.	Must you copy them?	Yes, I must.
15.	Have you copied them?	Yes, I have.
16.	What did you do?	I copied them.
17.	What must you do?	I must copy them.
18.	What have you done?	I've copied them.
19.	Isn't she going to go home?	Yes, she is.
20.	Wasn't she going home?	Yes, she was.
21.	Hadn't she better go home?	Yes, she'd better.
22.	What's she going to do?	She's going to go home.
23.	What was she doing?	She was going home.
24.	What had she better do?	She'd better go home.
25.	Shouldn't he speak English?	Yes, he should.
26.	Didn't he have to speak English?	Yes, he did.
27.	Couldn't he speak English?	Yes, he could.
28.	What should he do?	He should speak English.
29.	What did he have to do?	He had to speak English.
30.	What could he do?	He could speak English.

Conversation A

S1. Is that Mr. Brown's office?
S2. Yes, it is.
S1. Whose office is this?
S2. This office is Mr. Green's.

Conversation B

S1. Where's there a bus stop?
S2. I'm sorry. I didn't hear you.
S1. Is there a bus stop at the next corner?
S2. No, but there's a bus stop two blocks from here.

Conversation C

S1. Did the Italian students arrive here during the summer?
S2. No. They arrived here just a month ago.
S1. How long ago did the Greek students arrive?
S2. They arrived exactly two months ago.

Conversation D

S1. Did you paint your garage on Saturday?
S2. Yes. I painted the whole garage in three hours.
S1. What color did you paint it?
S2. I finally decided to paint it blue.

Conversation E

S1. Is Tom's dictionary around here anyplace?
S2. Yes. Tom's dictionary is over there on the table.
S1. Which one is Tom's—the red one or the blue one?
S2. The red one is his.

Exercise 1

1. They're studying.
   (??)

   What are they studying?
   They're studying their lessons.

2. She'll study.
   (??)

   What will she study?
   She'll study her lessons.

3. I studied.
   (??)

   What did you study?
   I studied my lessons.

4. He's studying.
   (??)

   What's he studying?
   He's studying his lessons.

5. They've studied.
   (??)

   What have they studied?
   They've studied their lessons.

6. I'm going to study.
   (??)

   What are you going to study?
   I'm going to study my lessons.

7. She can study.
   (??)

   What can she study?
   She can study her lessons.

8. He studies.
   (??)

   What does he study?
   He studies his lessons.

9. They must study.
   (??)

   What must they study?
   They must study their lessons.

10. I should study.
    (??)

    What should you study?
    I should study my lessons.

11. They were studying.
    (??)

    What were they studying?
    They were studying their lessons.

12. He used to study.
    (??)

    What did he use to study?
    He used to study his lessons.

13. She's supposed to study.
    (??)

    What's she supposed to study?
    She's supposed to study her lessons.

14. They'll study.
    (??)

    What will they study?
    They'll study their lessons.

15. I'd better study.
    (??)

    What had you better study?
    I'd better study my lessons.

16. They have to study.   What do they have to study?
    (??)   They have to study their lessons.

17. He's been studying.   What's he been studying?
    (??)   He's been studying his lessons.

18. We had to study.   What did you have to study?
    (??)   We had to study our lessons.

Exercise 2

1. I'll write at home.   Where will you write?
   (??)   I'll write at home.

2. I wrote my English lesson.   What did you write?
   (??)   I wrote my English lesson.

3. I must write for extra prac- Why must you write?
   tice.   I must write for extra prac-
   (??)   tice.

4. I should write in the eve-   When should you write?
   ning.   I should write in the evening.
   (??)

5. I've written to Mr. Brown.   Whom have you written to?
   (??)   I've written to Mr. Brown.

6. I write for extra practice.   Why do you write?
   (??)   I write for extra practice.

7. I'm going to write at home.   Where are you going to write?
   (??)   I'm going to write at home.

8. I used to write in the eve-   When did you use to write?
   ning.   I used to write in the evening.
   (??)

9. I'm writing for extra prac-   Why are you writing?
   tice.   I'm writing for extra practice.
   (??)

10. I have to write to Mr.   Whom do you have to write
    Brown.   to?
    (??)   I have to write to Mr. Brown.

11. I was writing my English lesson. (??)

What were you writing?
I was writing my English lesson.

12. I wrote for extra practice. (??)

Why did you write?
I wrote for extra practice.

13. I can write at home. (??)

Where can you write?
I can write at home.

14. I plan to write to Mr. (??)

Whom do you plan to write to?
I plan to write to Mr. Brown.

15. I'm writing for extra practice. (??)

Why are you writing?
I'm writing for extra practice.

16. I write in the evening. (??)

When do you write?
I write in the evening.

17. I've written my English lesson. (??)

What have you written?
I've written my English lesson.

18. I had to write at home. (??)

Where did you have to write?
I had to write at home.

Conversation A

S1. We should complain about the service in this store.
S2. Should we complain to one of the clerks?
S1. I don't think so.
S2. Whom should we complain to then?

Conversation B

S1. Have you chosen furniture for your apartment yet?
S2. No, we haven't.
S1. Why haven't you chosen any yet?
S2. Frankly, we just haven't had enough time.

Conversation C

S1. Does Mary have to go?
S2. Yes, she does. She has to go to the airport.
S1. How soon does she have to go?
S2. I'm not sure just how soon.

Conversation D

S1. Do you prefer this picture or that one?
S2. Of those two, I think I prefer the bottom one.
S1. Which one of the other two do you prefer?
S2. I really can't decide.

Conversation E

S1. I couldn't finish all the work yesterday.
S2. How come you couldn't finish it?
S1. Because I got started too late.
S2. Why don't you get started earlier next time?

Exercise 1

1.	What can he do?	He can write.
2.	What should he do?	He should write.
3.	What does he do?	He writes.
4.	What will he do?	He'll write.
5.	What's he doing?	He's writing.
6.	What must he do?	He must write.
7.	What's he done?	He's written.
8.	What did he do?	He wrote.
9.	What was he doing?	He was writing.
10.	What had he better do?	He'd better write.
11.	What's he going to do?	He's going to write.
12.	What does he plan to do?	He plans to write.
13.	What could he do?	He could write.
14.	What did he have to do?	He had to write.
15.	What should he have done?	He should have written.
16.	What did he use to do?	He used to write.

Exercise 2

1.	They'll write something.	What will they write?
2.	They were writing something.	What were they writing?
3.	They write something.	What do they write?
4.	They've written something.	What have they written?
5.	They're going to write something.	What are they going to write?
6.	They should write something.	What should they write?
7.	They can write something.	What can they write?
8.	They wrote something.	What did they write?
9.	They must write something.	What must they write?
10.	They're writing something.	What are they writing?
11.	They plan to write something.	What do they plan to write?
12.	They used to write something.	What did they use to write?
13.	They could have written something.	What could they have written?
14.	They'd better write something.	What had they better write?

Exercise 3

1. He can write.   Where?   Where can he write?

                          At home   He can write at home.

2. He should write.   How much?   How much should he write?

                          Two pages   He should write two pages.

3. He writes.   When?   When does he write?

                          In the morning   He writes in the morning.

4. He'll write.   What?   What will he write?

                          A short report   He'll write a short report.

5. He's writing.   To whom?   To whom is he writing?

                          Mr. Brown   He's writing to Mr. Brown.

6. He must write.   Why?   Why must he write?

                          To apply for a job He must write to apply for a job.

7. He's written.   How often?   How often has he written?

                          Every six months   He's written every six months.

8. He wrote.   Which one?   Which one did he write?

                          The long one   He wrote the long one.

9. He was writing.

What for?

What was he writing for?

Because he had to

He was writing because he had to.

10. He'd better write.

When?

When had he better write?

Tonight

He'd better write tonight.

11. He's going to write.

What?

What's he going to write?

A letter

He's going to write a letter.

12. He plans to write.

To whom?

To whom does he plan to write?

Mary

He plans to write to Mary.

13. He could write.

How much?

How much could he write?

Only two pages

He could write only two pages.

14. He had to write.

Why?

Why did he have to write?

To satisfy them

He had to write to satisfy them.

15. He should write.

What?

What should he write?

An apology

He should write an apology.

16 He used to write.

How often?

How often did he use to write?

Once a month

He used to write once a month.

Exercise 4

1. Did he take that one?
   Which one?
   (??)

   Which one did he take?
   He took that one.

2. Is Bill going to the movies
   now?
   Where?
   (??)

   Where's Bill going now?
   He's going to the movies now.

3. Wasn't it there because of
   that?
   Why?
   (??)

   Why wasn't it there?
   It wasn't there because of
   that.

4. Should we complain to the
   manager?
   Whom?

   (??)

   Whom should we complain
   to?
   We should complain to the
   manager.

5. Couldn't you get to Boston
   because of that?
   Why?

   (??)

   Why couldn't you get tc Boston?
   I couldn't get to Boston because of that.

6. Did he come here four
   months ago?
   How long ago?

   (??)

   How long ago did he come
   here?
   He came here four months
   ago.

7. Does she want her tea with
   cream?
   How?
   (??)

   How does she want her tea?
   She wants her tea with cream.

8. Is there a bus stop at the
    next corner?
    Where?   Where's there a bus stop?
    (??)   There's a bus stop at the next
                                        corner.

9. Should we buy groceries
    today?
    What?   What should we buy today?
    (??)   We should buy groceries
                                        today.

10. Did they use to get there
    by bus?
    How?   How did they use to get
                                        there?
    (??)   They used to get there by
                                        bus.

11. Did you have to travel for
    business reasons?
    Why?   Why did you have to travel?
    (??)   I had to travel for business
                                        reasons.

Conversation A

S1. Have you found a picture for your room yet?
S2. Yes. I was lucky enough to find one yesterday.
S1. Have you put it on the wall yet?
S2. No, but I'm going to put it up this afternoon.

Conversation B

S1. Have you heard about Robert's bad luck?
S2. No. What happened to him?
S1. I hear he's lost his job.
S2. You can't believe everything you hear.

Conversation C

S1. Someone stole money from the company last month.
S2. Some money was stolen two months ago too.
S1. I think the person who's stealing money will be caught.
S2. John said he thought the police would catch the thief soon.

Conversation D

S1. Did you bring your umbrella today?
S2. No, but I brought my tan raincoat.
S1. Maybe Fred will lend me his umbrella.
S2. I think he's already lent his to someone.

Conversation E

S1. Have you ridden in Fred's new car yet?
S2. Yes, I have. I rode in it last night.
S1. Did Fred let you drive the car?
S2. Yes. I drove it around the block a couple of times.

Exercise 1

1. Did you write the letter?

   Yes, I did. I wrote it yesterday.

2. Did he drive the car?

   Yes, he did. He drove it yesterday.

3. Did they do the work?

   Yes, they did. They did it yesterday.

4. Did she send the report?

   Yes, she did. She sent it yesterday.

5. Did you bring your money?

   Yes, I did. I brought it yesterday.

6. Did he read the article?

   Yes, he did. He read it yesterday.

7. Did she begin her work?

   Yes, she did. She began it yesterday.

8. Did they see the display?

   Yes, they did. They saw it yesterday.

9. Did he wear his raincoat?

   Yes, he did. He wore it yesterday.

10. Did you buy the bicycle?

    Yes, I did. I bought it yesterday.

11. Did they hold the meeting?

    Yes, they did. They held it yesterday.

12. Did she take the package?

    Yes, she did. She took it yesterday.

13. Did she quit her job?

    Yes, she did. She quit it yesterday.

14. Did he cut the rope?

    Yes, he did. He cut it yesterday.

15. Did they draw the diagram?

    Yes, they did. They drew it yesterday.

16. Did she get the message?

    Yes, she did. She got it yesterday.

Exercise 2

1. I forgot something yesterday.

   Have you forgotten anything today?

2. I lost something yesterday.

   Have you lost anything today?

3. I began something yesterday.

Have you begun anything today?

4. I sold something yesterday.

Have you sold anything today?

5. I made something yesterday.

Have you made anything today?

6. I took something yesterday.

Have you taken anything today?

7. I won something yesterday.

Have you won anything today?

8. I did something yesterday.

Have you done anything today?

9. I read something yesterday.

Have you read anything today?

10. I wrote something yesterday.

Have you written anything today?

11. I built something yesterday.

Have you built anything today?

12. I sent something yesterday.

Have you sent anything today?

13. I broke something yesterday.

Have you broken anything today?

14. I brought something yesterday.

Have you brought anything today?

15. I tore something yesterday.

Have you torn anything today?

16. I drew something yesterday.

Have you drawn anything today?

Exercise 3

1. You do that work well.

You've always done that work well.

2. The girl writes accurately.

She's always written accurately.

3. The man tells funny jokes.

He's always told funny jokes.

4. Those men drive carelessly.

They've always driven carelessly.

5. He gives money to charity.

He's always given money to charity.

6. Tom sends reports to them.

He's always sent reports to them.

7. The meetings begin on time.

They've always begun on time.

8. The motor runs very smoothly.

It's always run very smoothly.

9. She chooses clothes carefully.

She's always chosen clothes carefully.

10. John reads the daily reports.

He's always read the daily reports.

11. You forget people's names.

You've always forgotten people's names.

12. Mary has trouble with that.

She's always had trouble with that.

13. That man speaks rapidly.

He's always spoken rapidly.

14. I take good care of my car.

I've always taken good care of my car.

15. You eat breakfast very early.

You've always eaten breakfast very early.

16. That man wears a hat to work.

He's always worn a hat to work.

Exercise 4

1. Has the man ever seen it?   Yes. He saw it yesterday.
2. Have you broken one?   Yes. I broke one yesterday.
3. Has Mary ever worn one?   Yes. She wore one yesterday.
4. Have the men heard it?   Yes. They heard it yesterday.
5. Has the leader begun yet?   Yes. He began yesterday.
6. Have you ever driven one?   Yes. I drove one yesterday.
7. Has your sister eaten there?   Yes. She ate there yesterday.
8. Have the workers done it?   Yes. They did it yesterday.
9. Have they ever sung it?   Yes. They sang it yesterday.
10. Has Mr. White sent it?   Yes. He sent it yesterday.
11. Have the people read it?   Yes. They read it yesterday.
12. Has John made one?   Yes. He made one yesterday.
13. Has the girl bought one?   Yes She bought one yesterday.
14. Have you spoken to him?   Yes. I spoke to him yesterday.

Conversation A

S1. Did you sell those people your house?
S2. Yes. We finally sold it to them last week.
S1. Have they given you the money yet?
S2. Yes. They gave it to us just this morning.

Conversation B

S1. Has Robert chosen a new suit yet?
S2. Yes. He chose a very nice one on Saturday.
S1. Has he worn his new suit yet?
S2. Yes. He wore it to the meeting yesterday.

Conversation C

S1. Did Alice shut the window?
S2. Yes. She shut it a short time ago.
S1. She forgot it this morning.
S2. No. She left it open on purpose.

Conversation D

S1. Did you read the magazine?
S2. Yes. We read it this morning.
S1. Did you find the article I told you about?
S2. We found it all right, but you didn't tell us it was so long.

Conversation E

S1. Have you gone over that reading selection yet?
S2. Yes. I went over it last weekend.
S1. Did you understand everything in the essay?
S2. I think I understood all the important parts.

Conversation Drill A

S1. Where did you ____(A)____ the package?

S2. I ____(B)____ it in the closet.

S1. Would you please ____(C)____ it?

S2. I've ____(D)____ it already.

(A)	(B)	(C)	(D)
leave	left	open	opened
find	found	unwrap	unwrapped
set	set	move	moved
lay	laid	examine	examined
put	put	return	returned
hide	hid	inspect	inspected
see	saw	deliver	delivered
keep	kept	address	addressed

Conversation Drill B

S1. What's the matter?

S2. We've ____(A)____

S1. We haven't ____(B)____ yet.

S2. I'm very surprised.

(A)	(B)
spent our money	spent ours
chosen a name	chosen one
seen that movie	seen it
had some food	had any
bought a ticket	bought one
read the papers	read them
done something	done anything
taken that course	taken it

Conversation Drill A

S1. What's on your mind?

S2. Why did you ___(A)___ that?

S1. I ___(B)___ that because it was necessary.

S2. Of course, you know I haven't ___(C)___ one yet.

(A)	(B)	(C)
begin	began	begun
take	took	taken
read	read	read
choose	chose	chosen
do	did	done
write	wrote	written
draw	drew	drawn
see	saw	seen

Conversation Drill B

S1. Have you ever ___(A)___ one?

S2. Yes. In fact, I ___(B)___ one last week.

S1. I'm going to ___(C)___ one soon.

S2. John is ___(D)___ one right now.

(A)	(B)	(C)	(D)
written	wrote	write	writing
read	read	read	reading
worn	wore	wear	wearing
driven	drove	drive	driving
done	did	do	doing
given	gave	give	giving
brought	brought	bring	bringing
taken	took	take	taking

Conversation Drill A

S1. I like this   (A)   very much.
S2. Did you see the other   (A)   ?
S1. Yes, but this   (A)   is   (B)   than the other one.
S2. I think it's   (B)   too.

(A)	(B)
chair	more comfortable
color	prettier
suitcase	more practical
sweater	warmer
sports car	less conservative
silverware	more modern
television set	better
refrigerator	more convenient

Conversation Drill B

S1. Did you like the last one we saw?
S2. Yes, I did. It's certainly very   (A)   .
S1. It's as   (A)   as the first one, don't you think?
S2. In my opinion, it's   (B)   of all.

(A)	(B)
strong	the strongest
accurate	the most accurate
pretty	the prettiest
useful	the most useful
big	the biggest
unusual	the most unusual
comfortable	the most comfortable
nice	the nicest

Conversation Drill A

S1. I think John is quite ___(A)___ .
S2. I've noticed he's doing things ___(B)___ .
S1. John is always ___(C)___ than the others.
S2. I know he always does things more ___(B)___ than I do.

(A)	(B)	(C)
patient	patiently	more patient
quick	quickly	quicker
accurate	accurately	more accurate
deliberate	deliberately	more deliberate
slow	slowly	slower
awkward	awkwardly	more awkward
neat	neatly	neater
thorough	thoroughly	more thorough

Conversation Drill B

S1. Isn't Mr. Black a ___(A)___ person?
S2. Yes. He's certainly ___(B)___ than his brother.
S1. In my opinion, he's the ___(C)___ person in the group.
S2. He certainly speaks more ___(D)___ than the present chairman.

(A)	(B)	(C)	(D)
wise	wiser	wisest	wisely
confident	more confident	most confident	confidently
calm	calmer	calmest	calmly
earnest	more earnest	most earnest	earnestly
brave	braver	bravest	bravely
cautious	more cautious	most cautious	cautiously
kind	kinder	kindest	kindly
sensible	more sensible	most sensible	sensibly

Conversation A

S1. It's cold outside; I'm going to put on a sweater.
S2. You'd better put a coat on too.
S1. Yes, but we'd better take off our things when we're inside.
S2. We can take them off in the hall and hang them up.

Conversation B

S1. Bill found out his application was turned down.
S2. Who turned it down, and how did he find out?
S1. The membership committee turned down his application.
S2. Oh, I see. Then he found out the answer from the secretary.

Conversation C

S1. Did you take down the man's instructions?
S2. Yes. Do you want to look them over?
S1. Yes, please. I want to carry out his instructions as well as
     possible.
S2. All right. Let's sit down and go over them together.

Conversation D

S1. Did you throw away the extra paper?
S2. No. I gave about half of it away.
S1. Do you have some left then?
S2. No. I used up all the rest yesterday.

Conversation E

S1. Have you gone through the reports yet?
S2. No, I haven't. They were turned in just last night.
S1. Why don't you pick out a few for me to read then?
S2. I think I'll do that. I can use the help.

Exercise 1

1. We'll think over the plan carefully.   We'll think it over carefully.
2. I've turned in the reports.   I've turned them in.
3. Didn't she make out the form?   Didn't she make it out?
4. Why can't I find out those things?   Why can't I find them out?
5. Please don't point out the mistake.   Please don't point it out.
6. It's hard to break in new employees.   It's hard to break them in.
7. When did you use up the supplies?   When did you use them up?
8. You'd better put on your sweater.   You'd better put it on.
9. He couldn't take out those parts.   He couldn't take them out.
10. Why won't she bring up the subject?   Why won't she bring it up?
11. You're going to wear out your suit.   You're going to wear it out.
12. It's necessary to look up the words.   It's necessary to look them up.
13. Didn't he carry out their instructions?   Didn't he carry them out?
14. I've already worked out a plan.   I've already worked it out.
15. Please turn over your papers now.   Please turn them over now.
16. Shouldn't you throw away that rubbish?   Shouldn't you throw it away?
17. The weather held up our flight.   The weather held it up.
18. We'd better turn off the radio now.   We'd better turn it off now.
19. Please put away the tools before leaving.   Please put them away before leaving.

Exercise 2

1. Someone took it back. — It was taken back.
2. No one will try them out. — They won't be tried out.
3. Someone has used them up. — They've been used up.
4. No one is taking it down. — It isn't being taken down.
5. Someone ought to pick them out. — They ought to be picked out.
6. No one will turn that down. — That won't be turned down.
7. Someone was looking them over. — They were being looked over.
8. Someone is going to hold that up. — That's going to be held up.
9. No one should bring it up. — It shouldn't be brought up.
10. Someone has thrown them away. — They've been thrown away.
11. No one has to clear that up — That doesn't have to be cleared up.
12. Someone is giving them away. — They're being given away.
13. No one was pointing that out. — That wasn't being pointed out.
14. Someone will hand them in. — They'll be handed in.
15. Someone crossed it out. — It was crossed out.
16. No one is taking them off. — They aren't being taken off.

Conversation Drill A

S1. What did you say?
S2. Would you please ___(A)___ ?
S1. I ___(B)___ this morning.
S2. Sorry. I didn't realize that.

(A)	(B)
turn off the lights	turned them off
look over the report	looked it over
cross out those names	crossed them out
figure out the total cost	figured it out
look up those words	looked them up
bring up that matter	brought it up
take down the information	took it down
throw away those papers	threw them away

Conversation Drill B

S1. What are you thinking about?
S2. I guess we'll have to ___(A)___.
S1. Exactly why do you have to ___(B)___
S2. Because it's obviously important.

(A)	(B)
think over the plan	think it over
turn in the reports	turn them in
make out the form	make it out
point out the mistakes	point them out
bring up the subject	bring it up
carry out instructions	carry them out
look up the answer	look it up
turn over the papers	turn them over

Conversation A

S1. That isn't your jacket, is it?
S2. No, it isn't, but it looks like mine.
S1. But these are your gloves, aren't they?
S2. Yes, they are.

Conversation B

S1. There were a lot of people at the reception, weren't there?
S2. Yes, there were. Over 100, I'd guess.
S1. There wasn't enough food for everyone, was there?
S2. No, there wasn't, and everyone complained.

Conversation C

S1. It rains a lot in this part of the country, doesn't it?
S2. Yes, it does, but only in the spring.
S1. But it doesn't ever snow around here, does it?
S2. No, it never does.

Conversation D

S1. You left the office very late, didn't you?
S2. Yes, I did. Around eleven o'clock.
S1. Then you didn't get much sleep, did you?
S2. No, I didn't.

Conversation E

S1. John has been looking for a job, hasn't he?
S2. Yes, he has. Quite diligently too.
S1. He hasn't found a suitable one yet, has he?
S2. No, he hasn't, but I'm sure he will soon.

Exercise 1 / Line A1 /

That isn't your jacket.	That isn't your jacket, is it?
Those aren't your gloves.	Those aren't your gloves, are they?
This isn't your coat.	This isn't your coat, is it?
These aren't your shoes.	These aren't your shoes, are they?
That isn't your hat.	That isn't your hat, is it?
Those aren't your books.	Those aren't your books, are they?

Exercise 2 / Lines A1 and A3 /

That's your jacket.	That's your jacket, isn't it?
Those are your gloves.	Those are your gloves, aren't they?
This is your coat.	This is your coat, isn't it?
These are your shoes.	These are your shoes, aren't they?
That's your hat.	That's your hat, isn't it?
Those are your books.	Those are your books, aren't they?

Exercise 3 / Lines A1–A4 /

That's your jacket, isn't it?	Yes, it is.
That isn't your coat, is it?	No, it isn't.
Those are your gloves, aren't they?	Yes, they are.
Those aren't your books, are they?	No, they aren't.
This is your hat, isn't it?	Yes, it is.
These aren't your shoes, are they?	No, they aren't.

Exercise 4 / Lines A1–A4 /

1. Those are your books.
   (?)
   Those are your books, aren't they?
   Yes, they are. They're my books.

2. That isn't your jacket.
   (?)
   That isn't your jacket, is it?
   No, it isn't. It isn't my jacket.

3. That's your hat.
   (?)
   That's your hat, isn't it?
   Yes, it is. It's my hat.

4. Those aren't your gloves.

   (?)
   Those aren't your gloves, are they?
   No, they aren't. They aren't my gloves.

5. These are your shoes.
   (?)
   These are your shoes, aren't they?
   Yes, they are. They're my shoes.

Exercise 5 / Line C1 /

It rains a lot here.	It rains a lot here, doesn't it?
The men worked there.	The men worked there, didn't they?
John likes television.	John likes television, doesn't he?
The wind blew very hard.	The wind blew very hard, didn't it?
The girls enjoy that class.	The girls enjoy that class, don't they?
That caused the trouble.	That caused the trouble, didn't it?

Exercise 6 / Line C3 /

It doesn't rain much here.	It doesn't rain much here, does it?
The men didn't work there.	The men didn't work there, did they?
John doesn't like television.	John doesn't like television, does he?
The wind didn't blow hard.	The wind didn't blow hard, did it?
The girls don't enjoy the class.	The girls don't enjoy the class, do they?

Exercise 7 / Lines C1–C3 /

It rains a lot here, doesn't it?	Yes, it does.
The girls don't enjoy the class, do they?	No, they don't.
That caused the trouble, didn't it?	Yes, it did.
The men didn't work there, did they?	No, they didn't.
The wind blew hard, didn't it?	Yes, it did.
John doesn't like television, does he?	No, he doesn't.

Exercise 8 / Lines A1–A4 and C1–C3 /

They work hard, don't they?	Yes, they do.
They're working hard, aren't they?	Yes, they are.
They don't work hard, do they?	No, they don't.
They aren't working hard, are they?	No, they aren't.

She writes letters, doesn't she?	Yes, she does.
She's writing letters, isn't she?	Yes, she is.
She doesn't write letters, does she?	No, she doesn't.
She isn't writing letters, is she?	No, she isn't.

Exercise 9 / Lines C1–C3 /

1. The girls enjoy that class.

   (?)

   The girls enjoy that class, don't they?

   Yes, they do. They enjoy that class.

2. The men didn't work there.

   (?)

   The men didn't work there, did they?

   No, they didn't. They didn't work there.

3. The wind blew very hard.

   (?)

   The wind blew very hard, didn't it?

   Yes, it did. It blew very hard.

4. John doesn't like television.

   (?)

   John doesn't like television, does he?

   No, he doesn't. He doesn't like television.

5. It rains a lot here.
   (?)

   It rains a lot here, doesn't it?
   Yes, it does. It rains a lot here.

6. That didn't cause the trouble.
   (?)

   That didn't cause the trouble, did it?
   No, it didn't. It didn't **cause** the trouble.

Conversation A

S1.   There haven't been any storms recently, have there?
S2.   No, there haven't, but it's hard to believe.
S1.   I suppose we could get one anytime now, couldn't we?
S2.   We certainly could. This is the season.

Conversation B

S1.   Not many people in that office speak English, do they?
S2.   No, they don't, but all of them are taking classes now.
S1.   According to the rules, all employees have to learn it now,
       don't they?
S2.   Yes, they all do, and it's a problem.

Conversation C

S1.   She's already told John she'd like to go, hasn't she?
S2.   Yes, she has.
S1.   I guess we should plan on it then, shouldn't we?
S2.   Yes, we'd better, I think.

Conversation D

S1.   You hadn't ever seen the Ambassador before last night, had
       you?
S2.   No, I hadn't, although I did see John's pictures of him in
       May.
S1.   You could have met him at the last conference, couldn't you?
S2.   Yes, I could have, but I lost my nerve at the last moment.

Conversation E

S1.   We'd better tell someone about this, hadn't we?
S2.   Yes, I guess we'd better, but who?
S1.   The director wouldn't be very sympathetic, would he?
S2.   No. I'm afraid he wouldn't.

Exercise 1

1. It isn't raining now.   It isn't raining now, is it?
2. John didn't read that.   John didn't read that, did he?
3. The girls weren't ready.   The girls weren't ready, were they?
4. The people haven't seen it.   The people haven't seen it, have they?
5. There weren't any mistakes.   There weren't any mistakes, were there?
6. They won't try that.   They won't try that, will they?
7. She can't come tomorrow.   She can't come tomorrow, can she?
8. Mary doesn't enjoy that.   Mary doesn't enjoy that, does she?
9. Those aren't your books.   Those aren't your books, are they?
10. He didn't go to the lecture.   He didn't go to the lecture, did he?
11. You haven't done that yet.   You haven't done that yet, have you?
12. Mary doesn't walk to work.   Mary doesn't walk to work, does she?
13. There wasn't enough food left.   There wasn't enough food left, was there?
14. The train hasn't arrived yet.   The train hasn't arrived yet, has it?
15. The men couldn't help him.   The men couldn't help him, could they?
16. They aren't working now.   They aren't working now, are they?

Exercise 2

1. The man can help us.   The man can help us, can't he?
2. Mary lives near your house.   Mary lives near your house, doesn't she?
3. The boys are studying now.   The boys are studying now, aren't they?
4. John waited for his friend.   John waited for his friend, didn't he?

5. They'll be at the confer-   They'll be at the conference,
ence.   won't they?

6. There was enough coffee.   There was enough coffee,
wasn't there?

7. The girl saw the movie.   The girl saw the movie, didn't
she?

8. Students should study hard.   Students should study hard,
shouldn't they?

9. You're going to leave soon.   You're going to leave soon,
aren't you?

10. He usually rides on the   He usually rides on the bus,
bus.   doesn't he?

11. They went home quite late.   They went home quite late,
didn't they?

12. You've done that lesson.   You've done that lesson,
haven't you?

13. You'll be able to do that.   You'll be able to do that,
won't you?

14. They had trouble with it.   They had trouble with it,
didn't they?

15. That's your briefcase.   That's your briefcase, isn't it?

16. He has to work tonight.   He has to work tonight,
doesn't he?

Exercise 3

1. The men are working   The men are working now, aren't
now.   they?
(?)   Yes, they are. They're working
now.

2. John didn't read that.   John didn't read that, did he?
(?)   No, he didn't. He didn't read that.

3. The girl writes care-   The girl writes carefully, doesn't
fully.   she?
(?)   Yes, she does. She writes carefully.

4. It isn't raining now.   It isn't raining now, is it?
(?)   No, it isn't. It isn't training now.

5. They've seen the movie.

    (?)

They've seen the movie, haven't they?

Yes, they have. They've seen the movie.

6. The man can help us.

    (?)

The man can help us, can't he?

Yes, he can. He can help us.

7. Mary didn't wait for you.

    (?)

Mary didn't wait for you, did she?

No, she didn't. She didn't wait for me.

8. You've done that lesson.

    (?)

You've done that lesson, haven't you?

Yes, I have. I've done that lesson.

9. He didn't leave early.

    (?)

He didn't leave early, did he?

No, he didn't. He didn't leave early.

10. They should try that.

    (?)

They should try that, shouldn't they?

Yes, they should. They should try that.

11. She doesn't walk to work.

    (?)

She doesn't walk to work, does she?

No, she doesn't. She doesn't walk to work.

12. John went home late.

    (?)

John went home late, didn't he?

Yes, he did. He went home late.

13. Those aren't his books.

    (?)

Those aren't his books, are they?

No, they aren't. They aren't his books.

14. She's going to practice.

    (?)

She's going to practice, isn't she?

Yes, she is. She's going to practice.

15. You'll be at the meeting.

    (?)

You'll be at the meeting, won't you?

Yes, I will. I'll be at the meeting.

Conversation A

S1. My friend can speak French.
S2. Alice can too.
S1. But my friend can't speak German.
S2. Alice can't either.

Conversation B

S1. We went to the concert last night.
S2. We did too.
S1. But we didn't get there on time.
S2. We didn't either.

Conversation C

S1. I met that government official from Japan.
S2. So did I.
S1. But I didn't meet his wife.
S2. Neither did I.

Conversation D

S1. They're going to go to the beach today.
S2. I am too.
S1. They're also going to go to the amusement park.
S2. So am I.

Conversation E

S1. We've already done that lesson.
S2. So have we.
S1. But we haven't done the other one yet.
S2. Neither have we.

Exercise 1

1.	He learned all the words.	We did too.
2.	They're copying the sentences.	We are too.
3.	You've watched that program.	We have too.
4.	She should accept the offer.	We should too.
5.	They can work at the library.	We can too.
6.	John found the answer	We did too.
7.	She studies every evening.	We do too.
8.	They had to be at the meeting.	We did too.
9.	You've read that novel.	We have too.
10.	He got very good results.	We did too.
11.	They can do that easily.	We can too.
12.	She's working on that part.	We are too.
13.	He'll speak to Mr. Wilson.	We will too.
14.	They're going to leave soon.	We are too.
15.	She enjoys that T.V. program.	We do too.
16.	He's written to the company.	We have too.
17.	He's writing to the company.	We are too.
18.	He writes lots of letters.	We do too.

Exercise 2

1.	We've enjoyed everything so far.	So have they.
2.	She's going to speak to you.	So are they.
3.	You helped him very much.	So did they.
4.	I knew all the answers.	So did they.
5.	She's doing the lesson now.	So are they.
6.	He can explain it to you.	So can they.
7.	We'll be at the meeting.	So will they.
8.	I have enough time for that.	So do they.
9.	She should come with us.	So should they.
10.	We have to leave quite early.	So do they.
11.	You've done well up to now.	So have they.
12.	He's going to walk to work.	So are they.
13.	I was quite worried about that.	So were they.
14.	We like to listen to music.	So do they.
15.	She's already read that book.	So have they.
16.	You can ride home with us.	So can they.
17.	We could wait for you.	So could they.
18.	She appreciates your help.	So do they.

Exercise 3

1.	He didn't follow the instructions.	I didn't either.
2.	They aren't working on that now.	I'm not either.
3.	She hasn't taken the course yet.	I haven't either.
4.	John doesn't often do that.	I don't either.
5.	They didn't mind the changes.	I didn't either.
6.	She can't understand that part.	I can't either.
7.	He isn't working very hard.	I'm not either.
8.	They won't be able to attend.	I won't either.
9.	She shouldn't try to do that.	I shouldn't either.
10.	John doesn't have to work.	I don't either.
11.	Mary hasn't heard anything yet.	I haven't either.
12.	They can't possibly go there.	I can't either.
13.	They don't believe his excuse.	I don't either.
14.	John wasn't at the meeting.	I wasn't either.
15.	They aren't ready to go yet.	I'm not either.
16.	They haven't had any trouble.	I haven't either.
17.	You won't have any trouble.	I won't either.
18.	She isn't watching that.	I'm not either.

Exercise 4

1.	We didn't read the article.	Neither did he.
2.	Mary hasn't seen that movie.	Neither has he.
3.	I'm not going to mention it.	Neither is he.
4.	You don't often try that.	Neither does he.
5.	We won't say anything to her.	Neither will he.
6.	I don't enjoy that kind of music.	Neither does he.
7.	I can't understand the lesson.	Neither can he.
8.	We haven't heard anything yet.	Neither has he.
9.	You don't have to stay here.	Neither does he.
10.	I'm not ready to leave yet.	Neither is he.
11.	She can't help them right now.	Neither can he.
12.	You shouldn't try to do that.	Neither should he.
13.	You didn't answer my question.	Neither did he.
14.	She won't be able to go tomorrow.	Neither will he.
15.	They aren't working right now.	Neither is he.
16.	They weren't at the conference.	Neither was he.
17.	They won't be at the concert.	Neither will he.
18.	We can't finish it on time.	Neither can he.

Conversation Drill A

S1. What do you think?
S2. I suspect that Mary ____(A)____
S1. I'm sure that John ____(B)____
S2. Let's ask them about it to be sure.

(A)	(B)
took many pictures	did too
can't avoid that	can't either
wants to change it	does too
wasn't aware of this	wasn't either
has to ask permission	does too
won't agree with us	won't either
is going to object	is too
couldn't attend	couldn't either

Conversation Drill B

S1. What's your opinion about him?
S2. It's quite clear that he ____(A)____
S1. ____(B)____ the other workers, I suspect.
S2. That's probably correct.

(A)	(B)
took the things	so did
didn't read the report	neither did
has seen something	so have
can't handle it	neither can
will object to that	so will
has to give it up soon	so do
isn't cooperating at all	neither are
wants something	so do

Conversation A

S1. Do they know his name?
S2. I don't think so. Do you?
S1. Of course. Don't you?
S2. Sure. It's Mr. Smith.

Conversation B

S1. Didn't the men finish the work?
S2. I don't think they did.
S1. Do they expect us to do it?
S2. I certainly hope they don't.

Conversation C

S1. I didn't have enough time to speak to Mr. Fox.
S2. Why didn't you?
S1. Because I had to leave quite early.
S2. So did I, but I had enough time.

Conversation D

S1. Not many people heard the lecture, and I didn't either.
S2. Well, I did, and so did Fred.
S1. Did Mary and John?
S2. I don't think they did.

Conversation E

S1. Did you go to work yesterday?
S2. No, I just couldn't.
S1. Why couldn't you?
S2. I didn't feel very well at all.

Exercise 1 / Lines A1 and A2 /

Do they know his name?	No. Do you?
Have they spoken to him?	No. Have you?
Did they meet him?	No. Did you?
Can they convince him?	No. Can you?
Will they be seeing him?	No. Will you?
Are they annoyed at him?	No. Are you?

Exercise 2 / Lines B1 and B2 /

Didn't the men finish the work?	I don't think they did.
Haven't the men finished the work?	I don't think they have.
Aren't the men finishing the work?	I don't think they are.
Won't the men finish the work?	I don't think they will.
Can't the men finish the work?	I don't think they can.
Weren't the men finishing the work?	I don't think they were.

Exercise 3 / Line B3 /

Do they expect us to do it?

want	Do they want us to do it?
advise	Do they advise us to do it?
urge	Do they urge us to do it?
intend	Do they intend us to do it?
wish	Do they wish us to do it?

Exercise 4 / Line D1 /

They didn't hear it.	I didn't either.
They haven't seen it.	I haven't either.
They won't be there.	I won't either.
They don't enjoy it.	I don't either.
They aren't studying now.	I'm not either.
They can't go with him.	I can't either.

Exercise 5 / Line D2 /

They heard it.	So did John.
They've seen it.	So has John.
They'll be there.	So will John.
They enjoy it.	So does John.
They're studying now.	So is John.
They can go with him.	So can John.

Exercise 6

1.	I'm quite hungry now.	Are you?	Aren't you?
2.	I work eight hours every day.	Do you?	Don't you?
3.	I could understand everything.	Could you?	Couldn't you?
4.	I went to the meeting.	Did you?	Didn't you?
5.	I was very uncomfortable.	Were you?	Weren't you?
6.	I studied the lesson carefully.	Did you?	Didn't you?
7.	I'll be at the meeting early.	Will you?	Won't you?
8.	I plan to meet the men.	Do you?	Don't you?
9.	I can leave almost any time.	Can you?	Can't you?
10.	I've seen that movie already.	Have you?	Haven't you?
11.	I have to go back very soon.	Do you?	Don't you?
12.	I'd like to go home early.	Would you?	Wouldn't you?

Exercise 7

1.	I don't do it.	Why don't you?	I do.
2.	I haven't done it.	Why haven't you?	I have.
3.	I won't do it.	Why won't you?	I will.
4.	I didn't do it.	Why didn't you?	I did.
5.	I wasn't doing it.	Why weren't you?	I was.
6.	I can't do it.	Why can't you?	I can.
7.	I'm not doing it.	Why aren't you?	I am.
8.	I wouldn't do it.	Why wouldn't you?	I would.
9.	I'm not going to do it.	Why aren't you?	I am.
10.	I don't plan to do it.	Why don't you?	I do.
11.	I haven't done it.	Why haven't you?	I have.
12.	I don't have to do it.	Why don't you?	I do.
13.	I wasn't doing it.	Why weren't you?	I was.
14.	I won't do it.	Why won't you?	I will.
15.	I don't do it.	Why don't you?	I do.
16.	I'm not going to do it.	Why aren't you?	I am.

Conversation A

S1. They won't be very busy, but we will.
S2. I will too, but my brother won't.
S1. We can't possibly go, but they can.
S2. My brother can too, but I can't.

Conversation B

S1. My friend writes his reports on Monday, but I don't.
S2. Mr. Johnson doesn't either.
S1. I don't have enough time on Monday, but my friend does.
S2. Apparently Mr. Johnson does too.

Conversation C

S1. Most of my friends will be at the meeting, but I won't.
S2. Neither will my sister, but I will if I have time.
S1. My friends didn't attend the last meeting, but I did.
S2. My sister did too, but I didn't.

Conversation D

S1. I haven't seen that movie yet.
S2. You really ought to.
S1. I plan to tomorrow.
S2. It's an excellent film in my opinion.

Conversation E

S1. I don't often visit museums, but I like to whenever possible.
S2. I've never visited the Modern Museum, but I plan to tomorrow.
S1. I can go with you tomorrow if you want me to.
S2. Fine. I'd be glad to have company.

Exercise 1 / Line A1 /

They'll be busy.	But I won't.
They won't be busy.	But I will.
They're studying now.	But I'm not.
They aren't studying now.	But I am.
They walk to the office.	But I don't.
They don't walk to the office.	But I do.
They're ready for that.	But I'm not.
They aren't ready for that.	But I am.
They waited for the girl.	But I didn't.
They didn't wait for the girl.	But I did.

Exercise 2 / Lines D3, E1, E2 /

I plan to see it tomorrow.	I plan to tomorrow.
I hope to see it tomorrow.	I hope to tomorrow.
I expect to see it tomorrow.	I expect to tomorrow.
I want to see it tomorrow.	I want to tomorrow.
I intend to see it tomorrow.	I intend to tomorrow.
I prefer to see it tomorrow.	I prefer to tomorrow.
I have to see it tomorrow.	I have to tomorrow.

Exercise 3 / Line D1 /

1. I haven't seen that movie yet.
   want   I want to see it soon.
   like   I'd like to see it soon.

2. I haven't heard that program yet.
   want   I want to hear it soon.
   like   I'd like to hear it soon.

3. I haven't eaten there yet.
   want   I want to eat there soon.
   like   I'd like to eat there soon.

4. I haven't tried that method yet.
   want   I want to try it soon.
   like   I'd like to try it soon.

5. I haven't bought the tickets yet.
   want   I want to buy them soon.
   like   I'd like to buy them soon

Exercise 4

1. They saw the parade, but John didn't see it.
They saw the parade, but John didn't.

2. They didn't take the course, but John took it.
They didn't take the course, but John did.

3. They're watching TV, but John isn't watching TV.
They're watching TV, but John isn't.

4. They've been to the museum, but John hasn't been there.
They've been to the museum, but John hasn't.

5. They aren't studying that lesson, but John is studying it.
They aren't studying that lesson, but John is.

3. They haven't done that part, but John has done it.
They haven't done that part, but John has.

7. They'll be at the meeting, but John won't be there.
They'll be at the meeting, but John won't.

8. They won't drive to the park, but John will drive there.
They won't drive to the park, but John will.

Exercise 5

1. Do John and you write reports?
He does, but I don't.

2. Have John and you seen the show?
He has, but I haven't.

3. Are John and you working on that?
He is, but I'm not.

4. Did John and you leave early?
He did, but I didn't.

5. Were John and you late today?
He was, but I wasn't.

6. Are John and you going to do it?
He is, but I'm not.

7. Do John and you have to go?
He does, but I don't.

8. Were John and you writing then?
He was, but I wasn't.

9. Could John and you understand him?
He could, but I couldn't.

10. Would John and you care to go?
He would, but I wouldn't.

11. Will John and you be there to-   He will, but I won't.
night?

12. Can John and you come with   He can, but I can't.
me?

13. Have John and you been there   He has, but I haven't.
yet?

14. Do John and you study at   He does, but I don't.
home?

15. Are John and you satisfied with   He is, but I'm not.
it?

16. Did John and you buy new   He did, but I didn't.
books?

Conversation A

S1. My friend doesn't work very hard.
S2. Do you?
S1. Of course I do.
S2. Well, I don't. I hate to work.

Conversation B

S1. I always try to be careful.
S2. I usually do too.
S1. Do you always check your work several times?
S2. I usually do, but once in a while, I don't.

Conversation C

S1. I finished my work on time.
S2. No one else did.
S1. That's not entirely true.
S2. You're right. John did too, didn't he?

Conversation D

S1. Don't you like to dance?
S2. Of course I do.
S1. Then why don't you come to the dance?
S2. I really can't.

Conversation E

S1. When can the manager see me?
S2. Can you come at eleven o'clock this morning?
S1. No, but I can any time after two.
S2. Then I'll put your name down for two thirty.

Exercise 1 / Lines A1 and A2 /

My friend doesn't work very hard.	Do you?
My friend can't go to the meeting.	Can you?
My friend won't be at the party.	Will you?
My friend hasn't read the article.	Have you?
My friend didn't write any letters.	Did you?
My friend isn't taking any courses.	Are you?

Exercise 2 / Lines A2 and A3 /

Do you work very hard?	Of course I do.
Can you go to the meeting?	Of course I can.
Will you be at the party?	Of course I will.
Have you read the article?	Of course I have.
Did you write any letters?	Of course I did.
Are you taking any courses?	Of course I am.

Exercise 3 / Lines A1 and A4 /

My friend works hard.	He works hard, but I don't.
My friend can go to the meeting.	He can go to the meeting, but I can't.
My friend will be at the party.	He'll be at the party, but I won't.
My friend has read the article.	He's read the article, but I haven't.
My friend writes letters.	He writes letters, but I don't.

Exercise 4 / Line A4 /

I hate to work.

enjoy	I enjoy working.
want	I want to work.
avoid	I avoid working.
refuse	I refuse to work.
put off	I put off working.
intend	I intend to work.
plan	I plan to work.
suggest	I suggest working.
promise	I promise to work.

Exercise 5

1. We don't own a car yet, but we hope to own one.

   We don't own a car yet, but we hope to.

2. Peter drives to school, but I can't afford to drive to school.

   Peter drives to school, but I can't afford to.

3. I haven't heard from John, but I expect to hear from him.

   I haven't heard from John, but I expect to.

4. She didn't finish all the work, but she's going to finish it.

   She didn't finish all the work, but she's going to.

5. He'd like to go with them, but he doesn't plan to go with them.

   He'd like to go with them, but he doesn't plan to.

6. They don't try very hard, but they ought to try hard.

   They don't try very hard, but they ought to.

7. We haven't taken it yet, but we really intend to take it.

   We haven't taken it yet, but we really intend to.

8. He doesn't smoke cigars, but he used to smoke cigars.

   He doesn't smoke cigars, but he used to.

9. I want to review the lesson because I need to review it.

   I want to review the lesson because I need to.

10. He didn't study yesterday because he didn't want to study.

    He didn't study yesterday because he didn't want to.

11. He has to stay home tonight, but we don't have to stay home.

    He has to stay home tonight, but we don't have to.

12. They'd like to do it today, but they won't be able to do it.

    They'd like to do it today, but they won't be able to.

13. I'm not going to go there, but I'd like to go there.

    I'm not going to go there, but I'd like to.

Conversation A

S1. I would like to finish everything today.
S2. Will you be able to?
S1. I think so.
S2. I hope so, because it's rather urgent.

Conversation B

S1. Didn't Mary finish the work?
S2. I don't think so.
S1. Does he expect us to finish it?
S2. I hope not.

Conversation C

S1. We should invite them, but we don't want to.
S2   I understand your problem.
S1. They're extremely boring, don't you think?
S2. I'm afraid so.

Conversation D

S1. Do you understand the instructions?
S2. I think I do.
S1. Does your friend Peter?
S2. No. He doesn't seem to.

Conversation E

S1. Why should I ask for permission to leave?
S2. Everyone has to.
S1. I don't have to.
S2. Yes, you do. Everyone does.

Exercise 1

1. They've left already.
   appear

   Have they left already?
   It appears so.

2. They won't return today.
   appear

   Won't they return today?
   It doesn't appear so.

3. They'll finish the work.
   think

   Will they finish the work?
   I think so.

4. They didn't take the books.
   think

   Didn't they take the books?
   I don't think so.

5. They were watching the game.
   believe

   Were they watching the game?
   I believe so.

6. They aren't studying now.
   believe

   Aren't they studying now?
   I don't believe so.

7. They haven't read the book.
   seem

   Haven't they read the book?

   It doesn't seem so.

8. They're going to leave soon.
   seem

   Are they going to leave soon?

   It seems so.

9. They'll finish the work on time.
   presume

   Will they finish the work on time?
   I presume so.

10. They can't afford a new car.
    think

    Can't they afford a new car?

    I don't think so.

11. They're guarding the money.
    hope

    Are they guarding the money?

    I hope so.

12. They agree with us.
    suppose

    Do they agree with us?
    I suppose so.

13. They've written the report.   Have they written the report?
    assume   I assume so.

14. They didn't ask questions.   Didn't they ask questions?
    think   I don't think so.

15. They can't assist their   Can't they assist their friend?
    friend.
    believe   I don't believe so.

16. They've offered their assist-   Have they offered their as-
    ance.   sistance?
    presume   I presume so.

Conversation A

S1. By whom is the telephone answered?
S2. The secretary usually answers it.
S1. Who opens the mail every day?
S2. It's opened by the office manager.

Conversation B

S1. Was the letter written yesterday?
S2. I'm sorry, I didn't hear you.
S1. Did anyone write the letter yesterday?
S2. I'm afraid not.

Conversation C

S1. Were the reports read by all the employees?
S2. Yes. Everyone in this office read them.
S1. I think the reports should be posted in a better place.
S2. Yes. Let's post them right by the door next time.

Conversation D

S1. Will the repair work be done on time?
S2. Yes. The men will do it tomorrow.
S1. Has the work been started yet?
S2. The men started it just this morning.

Conversation E

S1. The loud noise frightened us.
S2. We were frightened by the noise too.
S1. Has anyone investigated it?
S2. I don't think it's been investigated yet.

Exercise 1

1.	The reports were corrected.	Someone corrected them.
2.	The machine is inspected.	Someone inspects it.
3.	The students will be assisted.	Someone will assist them.
4.	The girl has been notified.	Someone has notified her.
5.	The men are being in-instructed.	Someone is instructing them.
6.	The mirror was broken.	Someone broke it.
7.	The letters will be examined.	Someone will examine them.
8.	Mr. Smith was warned.	Someone warned him.
9.	The work is being done.	Someone is doing it.
10.	The assignments are corrected.	Someone corrects them.
11.	The problem has been solved.	Someone has solved it.
12.	The message can be sent.	Someone can send it.
13.	The people were advised.	Someone advised them.
14.	Mrs. Brown will be invited.	Someone will invite her.
15.	The papers are being copied.	Someone is copying them.
16.	The motor can be repaired.	Someone can repair it.

Exercise 2

1.	Someone broke the mirror.	It was broken.
2.	Someone will examine the letters.	They'll be examined.
3.	Someone is instructing the men.	They're being instructed.
4.	Someone has solved the problem.	It's been solved.
5.	Someone inspects the machine.	It's inspected.
6.	Someone will invite the lady.	She'll be invited.
7.	Someone corrected the reports.	They were corrected.
8.	Someone can send the message.	It can be sent.
9.	Someone is copying the papers.	They're being copied.
10.	Someone has notified the man.	He's been notified.
11.	Someone will assist the students.	They'll be assisted.
12.	Someone warned the girl.	She was warned.
13.	Someone is doing the work.	It's being done.
14.	Someone can repair the motor.	It can be repaired.
15.	Someone advised the people.	They were advised.

Conversation A

S1. I was embarrassed by Peter's comments.
S2. His comments embarrassed me too.
S1. Why wasn't he warned not to say anything?
S2. He was. I warned him.

Conversation B

S1. Has the report been completed yet?
S2. Yes. It was completed yesterday.
S1. Who'll distribute the confidential staff copies?
S2. They'll probably be distributed by Mr. White.

Conversation C

S1. We were confused by the fast action.
S2. There were plenty of confused people at that moment.
S1. The action didn't confuse those two men over there.
S2. They never get confused over anything.

Conversation D

S1. Is much attention being given to that problem?
S2. Yes. The committee is devoting a lot of time to it.
S1. They aren't treating the matter lightly, are they?
S2. I'm quite sure the matter isn't being treated lightly.

Conversation E

S1. Who permitted you to leave early?
S2. The foreman gave us permission to leave.
S1. Why were you given permission to leave?
S2. Because we had finished all the work for the day.

Exercise 1

1. They were hidden.   Someone hid them.
   No one hid them.   They weren't hidden.

2. She hasn't been informed.   No one has informed her.
   Someone has informed her.   She's been informed.

3. I'm being deceived.   Someone is deceiving me.
   No one is deceiving me.   I'm not being deceived.

4. They won't be assisted.   No one will assist them.
   Someone will assist them.   They'll be assisted.

5. You could be accused.   Someone could accuse you.
   No one could accuse you.   You couldn't be accused.

6. We weren't complimented.   No one complimented us.
   Someone complimented us.   We were complimented.

7. That had to be admitted.   Someone had to admit that.
   No one had to admit that.   That didn't have to be admitted.

8. He isn't encouraged.   No one encourages him.
   Someone encourages him.   He's encouraged.

9. They were broken.   Someone broke them.
   No one broke them.   They weren't broken.

10. That didn't use to be done.   No one used to do that.
    Someone used to do that.   That used to be done.

11. We're being blamed.   Someone is blaming us.
    No one is blaming us.   We aren't being blamed.

12. You won't be embarrassed.   No one will embarrass you.
    Someone will embarrass you.   You'll be embarrassed.

13. They aren't advised.   No one advises them.
    Someone advises them.   They're advised.

14. It's been unwrapped.   Someone has unwrapped it.
    No one has unwrapped it.   It hasn't been unwrapped.

15. That mustn't be assumed.   No one must assume that.
    Someone must assume that.   That must be assumed.

Conversation Drill A

S1. Did John tell you the news?
S2. Yes. I hear that they _____(A)_____
S1. Why _____(B)_____ ?
S2. I really can't answer that.

(A)	(B)
are removing it	is it being removed
fastened them	were they fastened
had to translate it	did it have to be translated
have opposed it	has it been opposed
must return them	must they be returned
were considering it	was it being considered
will modify them	will they be modified
distributed it	was it distributed

Conversation Drill B

S1. Can you tell me who _____(A)_____ ?
S2. I know I didn't _____(B)_____ .
S1. I think _____(C)_____ last night.
S2. I still can't tell you who did it.

(A)	(B)	(C)
broke that glass	break it	it was broken
brought these boxes	bring them	they were brought
took that book	take it	it was taken
lost those tickets	lose them	they were lost
drove my car	drive it	it was driven
sent those letters	send them	they were sent
drank all the milk	drink it	it was drunk
did the work	do it	it was done

Conversation A

S1. Where's the public library?
S2. I beg your pardon.
S1. Can you tell me where the library is?
S2. Two blocks from here, on the right.

Conversation B

S1. How do you say that in English?
S2. I don't remember how you say that in English.
S1. Who can help us with this?
S2. Let's ask Pierre who can help us with it.

Conversation C

S1. Why were you absent?
S2. I can't tell you why I was absent.
S1. Where did you go?
S2. I can't tell you where I went either.

Conversation D

S1. Whom did Alice write to yesterday?
S2. She hasn't told me whom she wrote to.
S1. What did she write about?
S2. She hasn't told me what she wrote about either.

Conversation E

S1. What are they doing?
S2. I can't imagine what they're doing.
S1. When will they finish?
S2. I have no idea when they'll finish.

Exercise 1

1. I can tell you where they study. Where do they study?
2. I can tell you when they can study. When can they study?
3. I can tell you what they had to study. What did they have to study?
4. I can tell you what they've studied. What have they studied?
5. I can tell you how much they studied. How much did they study?
6. I can tell you where they're studying. Where are they studying?
7. I can tell you why they won't study. Why won't they study?
8. I can tell you when they're going to study. When are they going to study?
9. I can tell you what part they didn't study. What part didn't they study?
10. I can tell you where they usually study. Where do they usually study?
11. I can tell you which one they studied. Which one did they study?
12. I can tell you when they must study. When must they study?
13. I can tell you what they used to study. What did they use to study?
14. I can tell you how long they should study. How long should they study?
15. I can tell you where they've been studying. Where have they been studying?
16. I can tell you what they're going to study. What are they going to study?
17. I can tell you why they can't study. Why can't they study?
18. I can tell you which one they're studying. Which one are they studying?
19. I can tell you when they usually study. When do they usually study?
20. I can tell you which one they'd better study. Which one had they better study?

Exercise 2

1   Haven't you heard what she'll write? | No. What will she write?

2. Haven't you heard why she couldn't write? | No. Why couldn't she write?

3. Haven't you heard how often she writes? | No. How often does she write?

4. Haven't you heard where she's writing? | No. Where's she writing?

5. Haven't you heard what she's written? | No. What's she written?

6. Haven't you heard how much she wrote? | No. How much did she write?

7. Haven't you heard what she has to write? | No. What does she have to write?

8. Haven't you heard when she should write? | No. When should she write?

9. Haven't you heard whom she used to write to? | No. Whom did she use to write to?

10. Haven't you heard what she's going to write? | No. What's she going to write?

11. Haven't you heard how much she must write? | No. How much must she write?

12. Haven't you heard how long she was writing? | No. How long was she writing?

13. Haven't you heard when she usually writes? | No. When does she usually write?

14. Haven't you heard which one she'd better write? | No. Which one had she better write?

15. Haven't you heard where she's been writing? | No. Where's she been writing?

16. Haven't you heard what she's written? | No. What's she written?

17. Haven't you heard which one she's going to write? | No. Which one is she going to write?

18. Haven't you heard what she plans to write? | No. What does she plan to write?

19. Haven't you heard how much she wrote? | No. How much did she write?

Exercise 3

1.	Where will he be?	I don't know where he'll be.
2.	Why did she leave?	I don't know why she left.
3.	Who's that man?	I don't know who that man is.
4.	When did they return?	I don't know when they returned.
5.	Where's John going?	I don't know where John is going.
6.	Where does she live?	I don't know where she lives.
7.	When did they arrive?	I don't know when they arrived.
8.	When are they leaving?	I don't know when they are leaving.
9.	Why was she absent?	I don't know why she was absent.
10.	Why didn't she return?	I don't know why she didn't return.
11.	Why did Mary buy it?	I don't know why Mary bought it.
12.	Who's that tall man?	I don't know who that tall man is.
13.	Who's doing the work?	I don't know who's doing the work.
14.	Who wrote this paper?	I don't know who wrote this paper.
15.	Whom did they invite?	I don't know whom they invited.
16.	Whom should I speak to?	I don't know whom you should speak to.

Exercise 4

1.	Whose house is that?	Please tell us whose house that is.
2.	Whose book did he use?	Please tell us whose book he used.
3.	What happened to him?	Please tell us what happened to him.
4.	What's he talking about?	Please tell us what he's talking about.
5.	What does the word mean?	Please tell us what the word means.

6.	What do you call that?	Please tell us what you call that.
7.	What did she ask them?	Please tell us what she asked them.
8.	What country is he from?	Please tell us what country he is from.
9.	What cities did he visit?	Please tell us what cities he visited.
10.	Which one is Brown's?	Please tell us which one is Brown's.
11.	Which one does he want?	Please tell us which one he wants.
12.	Which does John prefer?	Please tell us which John prefers.
13.	How does it work?	Please tell us how it works.
14.	How old is Mr. Brown?	Please tell us how old Mr. Brown is.
15.	How much did it cost?	Please tell us how much it cost.
16.	How do you say this?	Please tell us how you say this.

Conversation A

S1. When did Peter return?
S2. I beg your pardon.
S1. Please tell me when Peter returned.
S2. I can't tell you.

Conversation B

S1. When will the party be held?
S2. Tom can tell you when the party will be held.
S1. Whom did they invite to the party?
S2. You'll have to ask Tom whom they invited.

Conversation C

S1. Where did the people go?
S2. I don't have any idea where they went.
S1. Do you know where John went?
S2. I didn't even know he had gone.

Conversation D

S1. What did Fred say to Mary?
S2. She didn't tell me what Fred had said to her.
S1. Where will she be this afternoon?
S2. She didn't tell me where she would be.

Conversation E

S1. Whose car is Paul using?
S2. He didn't tell me whose car he was using.
S1. Why does he need a car so urgently?
S2. Why he needs a car really doesn't interest me.

Exercise 1

1. Where do they study?	I really wonder where they study.
2. When can they study?	I really wonder when they can study.
3. What did they have to study?	I really wonder what they had to study.
4. What have they studied?	I really wonder what they've studied.
5. How much did they study?	I really wonder how much they studied.
6. Where are they studying?	I really wonder where they're studying.
7. Why won't they study?	I really wonder why they won't study.
8. When do they generally study?	I really wonder when they generally study.
9. What do they usually study?	I really wonder what they usually study.
10. When will they study?	I really wonder when they'll study.
11. When must they study?	I really wonder when they must study.
12. What did they use to study?	I really wonder what they used to study.
13. How long should they study?	I really wonder how long they should study.
14. Where have they been studying?	I really wonder where they've been studying.
15. What are they going to study?	I really wonder what they're going to study.
16. Why can't they study?	I really wonder why they can't study.
17. Which one are they studying?	I really wonder which one they're studying.
18. When do they usually study?	I really wonder when they usually study.
19. Which one had they better study?	I really wonder which one they'd better study.

Exercise 2

1. What will she write?

Haven't you heard what she'll write?

2. Why couldn't she write?

Haven't you heard why she couldn't write?

3. How often does she write?

Haven't you heard how often she writes?

4. Where's she writing?

Haven't you heard where she's writing?

5. What's she written?

Haven't you heard what she's written?

6. How much did she write?

Haven't you heard how much she wrote?

7. What does she have to write?

Haven't you heard what she has to write?

8. How much has she written?

Haven't you heard how much she's written?

9. Where's she going to write?

Haven't you heard where she's going to write?

10. Whom did she write to?

Haven't you heard whom she wrote to?

11. When should she write?

Haven't you heard when she should write?

12. Whom did she use to write to?

Haven't you heard whom she used to write to?

13. What's she going to write?

Haven't you heard what she's going to write?

14. How much must she write?

Haven't you heard how much she must write?

15. How long was she writing?

Haven't you heard how long she was writing?

16. When does she usually write?

Haven't you heard when she usually writes?

17. Which one had she better write?

Haven't you heard which one she'd better write?

18. Where's she been writing?

Haven't you heard where she's been writing?

19. What's she written?

Haven't you heard what she's written?

Exercise 3

1. Why did they wear it?
    Let's ask them.

    Let's ask them why they wore it.

2. Why did she choose it?
    Please tell me.

    Please tell me why she chose it.

3. Why did John make it?
    Can we find out?

    Can we find out why John made it?

4. Why did you write it?
    We all wonder.

    We all wonder why you wrote it.

5. Why did they bring it?
    Ask your friend.

    Ask your friend why they brought it.

6. Why did the man steal it?
    I can't imagine.

    I can't imagine why the man stole it.

7. Why did Tom hold it?
    No one can explain.

    No one can explain why Tom held it.

8. Why did Alice say it?
    He doesn't know.

    He doesn't know why Alice said it.

9. Why did they buy it?
    Will you ask them?

    Will you ask them why they bought it?

10. Why did she sell it?
    Has she told you?

    Has she told you why she sold it?

11. Why did the boy read it?
    Let's find out.

    Let's find out why the boy read it.

12. Why did they send it?
    John must realize.

    John must realize why they sent it.

13. Why did the boys break it?
    Do you have any idea?

    Do you have any idea why the boys broke it?

Exercise 4

1. Where's she going to stay?
   Don't you know?

   Don't you know where she's going to stay?

2. When do they plan to go?
   Please tell all of us.

   Please tell all of us when they plan to go.

3. Why hasn't he spoken to us?
   Let's ask him.

   Let's ask him why he hasn't spoken to us.

4. Where did they take it?
   Everyone wonders.

   Everyone wonders where they took it.

5. How can she possibly do it?
   No one can imagine.

   No one can imagine how she can possibly do it.

6. Which one will they use?
   Can we find out?

   Can we find out which one they'll use?

7. Why don't they want to go?
   Did you ask them?

   Did you ask them why they don't want to go?

8. Where does she study?
   Mary can tell you.

   Mary can tell you where she studies.

9. What did he pay for that?
   Do you remember?

   Do you remember what he paid for that?

10. Where have they all gone?
    Won't Tom know?

    Won't Tom know where they've all gone?

11. Why is that so difficult?
    We all wonder.

    We all wonder why that's so difficult.

12. How did he do that part?
    Can't he explain?

    Can't he explain how he did that part?

13. How much did the men have?
    No one remembers.

    No one remembers how much the men had.

Conversation A

S1. My friend enrolled at a local school.
S2. Did he say why he enrolled there?
S1. He enrolled there to improve his English, he said.
S2. I suspect he did it to satisfy his boss.

Conversation B

S1. I've come to see Alice.
S2. · Sorry. She left for the library about ten minutes ago.
S1. I wonder why she went there.
S2. I think she went there to meet someone.

Conversation C

S1. Could I borrow some money from you?
S2. What do you need it for?
S1. I need it to pay my telephone bill.
S2. All right, but I'll have to stop at the bank to get it.

Conversation D

S1. John has changed his plans in order to go with us.
S2. I'm glad that he was able to change them.
S1. In order to change them, he had to speak to Mr. White.
S2. It was nice of Mr. White to give John permission.

Conversation E

S1. I'm here to get some details about this classified ad.
S2. I'm sorry, but you'll have to write to the advertiser.
S1. Why must I write to the advertiser?
S2. In order to get the information you want.

Exercise 1

1. I enrolled in a course. I wanted to improve my English.

I enrolled in a course to improve my English.

2. He shut the window. He wanted to keep out the noise.

He shut the window to keep out the noise.

3. They questioned us. They wanted to find out the answer.

They questioned us to find out the answer.

4. She went to the store. She wanted to buy groceries.

She went to the store to buy groceries.

5. The boys ran fast. The boys wanted to get there on time.

The boys ran fast to get there on time.

6. I had to do that. I wanted to satisfy my boss.

I had to do that to satisfy my boss.

7. We went back later. We wanted to see it again.

We went back later to see it again.

8. Mary informed Mr. Brown. Mary wanted to hear his reaction.

Mary informed Mr. Brown to hear his reaction.

9. You called your friend. You wanted to get help.

You called your friend to get help.

10. His wife gave him a list. His wife wanted to remind him.

His wife gave him a list to remind him.

11. He went to bed early. He wanted to get additional rest.

He went to bed early to get additional rest.

12. I borrowed some money. I wanted to pay for the tickets.

I borrowed some money to pay for the tickets.

13. They stayed at home. They wanted to finish the report.

They stayed at home to finish the report.

14. She turned on the radio. She wanted to hear that program.

She turned on the radio to hear that program.

15. I'm going to open that window. I want to get some fresh air.

I'm going to open that window to get some fresh air.

16. They've taken an examination. They want to qualify for it.

They've taken an examination to qualify for it.

Exercise 2

1. He wants to go with them. He's changed his plans.

   He's changed his plans in order to go with them.

2. They want to open the box. They're using a knife.

   They're using a knife in order to open the box.

3. You want to attend it. You must make a reservation.

   You must make a reservation in order to attend it.

4. He wanted to get a raise. He had to study accounting.

   He had to study accounting in order to get a raise.

5. They wanted to get there on time. They drove very fast.

   They drove very fast in order to get there on time.

6. Mary wants to please them. Mary will do anything.

   Mary will do anything in order to please them.

7. I wanted to hear the man. I turned down the radio.

   I turned down the radio in order to hear the man.

8. He wants to save money. He does his own cooking.

   He does his own cooking in order to save money.

9. He wanted to surprise them. We kept everything a secret.

   We kept everything a secret in order to surprise them.

10. John wants to go to college. John must save his money.

    John must save his money in order to go to college.

11. We wanted to see the parade. We went downtown early.

    We went downtown early in order to see the parade.

12. I wanted to get more information. I went to the library.

    I went to the library in order to get more information.

13. She wants to go to Europe. She plans to quit her job.

    She plans to quit her job in order to go to Europe.

14. I want to finish all the work. I must start quite early.

    I must start quite early in order to finish all the work.

15. He wanted to improve his English. He practiced daily.

    He practiced daily in order to improve his English.

16. I wanted to get his address. I had to write to his mother.

    I had to write to his mother in order to get his address.

Conversation A

S1. Do you enjoy writing letters?
S2. No. I put off writing letters whenever possible.
S1. Do you also postpone writing reports?
S2. Unfortunately, I do.

Conversation B

S1. Why did they refuse to give you the information?
S2. They probably don't wish to reveal their plans yet.
S1. Did they seem to want to help us?
S2. Yes. In fact, they even offered to.

Conversation C

S1. Have you finished writing the report?
S2. I expect to complete it in an hour or so.
S1. Don't stop working because of me.
S2. I won't. I've resolved to finish it today.

Conversation D

S1. Have you practiced using the new words in sentences?
S2. No. I'm afraid I've failed to do that.
S1. I strongly advise practicing that way.
S2. The teacher suggested doing it that way too.

Conversation E

S1. What has Paul finally decided to become?
S2. I think he's considering becoming a lawyer.
S1. Where does he intend to go to school?
S2. So far, he's avoided making that decision.

Exercise 1

1. We hoped to see that. — What did you hope to see?
2. We considered seeing that. — What did you consider seeing?
3. We offered to see that. — What did you offer to see?
4. We discussed seeing that. — What did you discuss seeing?
5. We wished to see that. — What did you wish to see?
6. We appreciated seeing that. — What did you appreciate seeing?
7. We planned to see that. — What did you plan to see?
8. We failed to see that. — What did you fail to see?
9. We favored seeing that. — What did you favor seeing?
10. We postponed seeing that. — What did you postpone seeing?
11. We resolved to see that. — What did you resolve to see?
12. We stopped seeing that. — What did you stop seeing?
13. We demanded to see that. — What did you demand to see?
14. We kept on seeing that. — What did you keep on seeing?
15. We forgot to see that. — What did you forget to see?
16. We pretended to see that. — What did you pretend to see?

Exercise 2

1. postpone — What did you postpone seeing?
2. demand — What did you demand to see?
3. plan — What did you plan to see?
4. fail — What did you fail to see?
5. favor — What did you favor seeing?
6. consider — What did you consider seeing?
7. resolve — What did you resolve to see?
8. offer — What did you offer to see?
9. pretend — What did you pretend to see?
10. hope — What did you hope to see?
11. discuss — What did you discuss seeing?
12. appreciate — What did you appreciate seeing?
13. stop — What did you stop seeing?
14. wish — What did you wish to see?
15. forget — What did you forget to see?
16. keep on — What did you keep on seeing?

Conversation A

S1. When do you plan to leave for Hong Kong?
S2. We hope to leave on the tenth.
S1. Why did you put off leaving until the tenth?
S2. Well, we need to buy a lot of things before leaving.

Conversation B

S1. When do you expect to hear from your friends?
S2. I really hesitate even to guess.
S1. I advise not worrying about it.
S2. I've already made up my mind not to worry.

Conversation C

S1. Do you resent having to follow orders?
S2. Truthfully, I can't stand taking orders from people.
S1. But you shouldn't risk losing your job because of that.
S2. I try not to take chances.

Conversation D

S1. I can't help worrying about what they'll do.
S2. Personally, I don't think they'll dare do anything.
S1. I recall having heard other people say that.
S2. We can always force them to stop complaining.

Conversation E

S1. Did you warn your friend not to say anything?
S2. I told him it was important that he reveal nothing.
S1. I recommend that he even avoid answering any questions.
S2. I'll remind him to keep this a strict secret.

Exercise 1

1. She decided to do that.   What did she decide to do?
2. She avoided doing that.   What did she avoid doing?
3. She needed to do that.   What did she need to do?
4. She resisted doing that.   What did she resist doing?
5. She delayed doing that.   What did she delay doing?
6. She wanted to do that.   What did she want to do?
7. She practiced doing that.   What did she practice doing?
8. She disliked doing that.   What did she dislike doing?
9. She expected to do that.   What did she expect to do?
10. She finished doing that.   What did she finish doing?
11. She promised to do that.   What did she promise to do?
12. She suggested doing that.   What did she suggest doing?
13. She intended to do that.   What did she intend to do?
14. She advised doing that.   What did she advise doing?
15. She refused to do that.   What did she refuse to do?
16. She enjoyed doing that.   What did she enjoy doing?
17. She put off doing that.   What did she put off doing?
18. She offered to do that.   What did she offer to do?

Exercise 2

1. What did he want?   He wanted to do that.
2. What did he avoid?   He avoided doing that.
3. What did he refuse?   He refused to do that.
4. What did he finish?   He finished doing that.
5. What did he decide?   He decided to do that.
6. What did he promise?   He promised to do that.
7. What did he resist?   He resisted doing that.
8. What did he need?   He needed to do that.
9. What did he advise?   He advised doing that.
10. What did he practice?   He practiced doing that.
11. What did he suggest?   He suggested doing that.
12. What did he expect?   He expected to do that.
13. What did he delay?   He delayed doing that.
14. What did he enjoy?   He enjoyed doing that.
15. What did he intend?   He intended to do that.
16. What did he dislike?   He disliked doing that.
17. What did he offer?   He offered to do that.
18. What did he put off?   He put off doing that.

Exercise 3

1. It's essential to continue. — Continuing is essential.
2. It'll be important to start. — Starting will be important.
3. It hasn't been pleasant to work. — Working hasn't been pleasant.
4. It was necessary to succeed. — Succeeding was necessary.
5. It shouldn't be foolish to try. — Trying shouldn't be foolish.
6. It can be dangerous to proceed. — Proceeding can be dangerous.
7. It won't be absurd to go back. — Going back won't be absurd.
8. It was only sensible to apologize. — Apologizing was only sensible.
9. It isn't very fair to complain. — Complaining isn't very fair.
10. It'll be rather helpful to watch. — Watching will be rather helpful.
11. It's been very convenient to observe. — Observing has been very convenient.
12. It would be dishonest to compete. — Competing would be dishonest.
13. It must have been hard to choose. — Choosing must have been hard.
14. It won't be practical to go ahead. — Going ahead won't be practical.
15. It would have been selfish to stop. — Stopping would have been selfish.
16. It used to be impossible to rest. — Resting used to be impossible.
17. It's been delightful to travel. — Traveling has been delightful.
18. It must be wonderful to relax. — Relaxing must be wonderful.
19. It shouldn't have been hard to win. — Winning shouldn't have been hard.
20. It'll be quite unpleasant to wait. — Waiting will be quite unpleasant.

Exercise 4

1. It'll be interesting to observe that.

   Observing that will be interesting.

2. It's boring to memorize things.

   Memorizing things is boring.

3. It's been pleasing to have them.

   Having them has been pleasing.

4. It was thrilling to recall that.

   Recalling that was thrilling.

5. It can be annoying to hear that.

   Hearing that can be annoying.

6. It was satisfying to try it once.

   Trying it once was satisfying.

7. It's really astonishing to realize it.

   Realizing it is really astonishing.

8. It'll be amusing to watch them.

   Watching them will be amusing.

9. It must be amazing to compare them.

   Comparing them must be amazing.

10. It could be disturbing to see that.

    Seeing that could be disturbing.

11. It's irritating to put up with that.

    Putting up with that is irritating.

12. It'll be reassuring to examine them.

    Examining them will be reassuring.

13. It was shocking to comprehend that.

    Comprehending that was shocking.

14. It should be inspiring to attend one.

    Attending one should be inspiring.

15. It's been disappointing to find it out.

    Finding it out has been disappointing.

16. It's startling to see one suddenly.

    Seeing one suddenly is startling.

Conversation Drill A

S1.   I'll be in Europe by next week.
S2.   There are lots of things ___ *(A)* ___
S1.   I ___ *(B)* ___ as much as possible.
S2.   Have a good time!

(A)	*(B)*
to see there	hope to see
to do on the continent	plan to do
to enjoy in that area	want to enjoy
to take pictures of	expect to use my camera
to get interested in	intend to travel around

Conversation Drill B

S1.   Are you looking for me?
S2.   Yes. Have you finished ___ *(A)* ___ yet?
S1.   Just ___ *(B)* ___ .
S2.   Please try to finish everything by tonight.

(A)	*(B)*
filling out your application	the first two pages
writing your daily report	the essential details
looking over the figures	the important statistics
checking the two lists	the first one

Conversation Drill C

S1.   Why are you so unhappy about your assistant?
S2.   Well, she always ___ *(A)* ___
S1.   Does she ___ *(B)* ___ ?
S2.   I'm afraid she does.

(A)	*(B)*
avoids doing her share	want to find another job
advises changing everything	ever threaten to quit
postpones finishing her work	expect to be promoted
resists taking orders	ever refuse to take orders
puts off typing reports	fail to do her share

Conversation A

S1. Where should I park my car?
S2. Didn't Fred show you where to park it?
S1. He wasn't sure what to tell me.
S2. Then let's ask the guard over there where to put it.

Conversation B

S1. Would you explain how to pronounce this word?
S2. I thought you already knew how to pronounce it.
S1. I did know, but I've forgotten.
S2. Well, I hope you remember how to pronounce it next time.

Conversation C

S1. Whom should we see to get permission to leave?
S2. I think I know whom to speak to.
S1. I wonder how we can explain our difficult situation.
S2. I've been wondering how to do it too.

Conversation D

S1. Whom are you going to ride to the party with?
S2. Mary, because she knows where to go.
S1. I didn't realize Mary knew how to drive a car.
S2. I think she learned how to drive just recently.

Conversation E

S1. Which one of these sweaters are you going to buy?
S2. I really don't know which one to choose.
S1. In that case, do you want me to tell you what to do?
S2. Since I can't decide which to take, I'd appreciate your advice.

Exercise 1

We discovered how to do it.

when	We discovered when to do it.
wondered	We wondered when to do it.
where	We wondered where to do it.
decided	We decided where to do it.
what	We decided what to do.
knew	We knew what to do.
when	We knew when to do it.
learned	We learned when to do it.
what	We learned what to do.
explained	We explained what to do.
how	We explained how to do it.
remembered	We remembered how to do it.
when	We remembered when to do it.
forgot	We forgot when to do it.
what	We forgot what to do.

Exercise 2

1.	Where will he go?	He knows where to go.
2.	Which ones will they bring?	They know which ones to bring.
3.	How much will you pay?	I know how much to pay.
4.	When will she leave there?	She knows when to leave there.
5.	Whom will the man see?	He knows whom to see.
6.	What will John give them?	He knows what to give them.
7.	How will they find the man?	They know how to find the man.
8.	Which will you use last?	I know which to use last.
9.	How far will she drive?	She knows how far to drive.
10.	What kind will he choose?	He knows what kind to choose.
11.	Which one will they talk about?	They know which one to talk about.
12.	Where will she get the money?	She knows where to get the money.
13.	What will they refer to?	They know what to refer to.

Conversation A

S1. Is it possible to convince your friend he's wrong?
S2. Well, he's likely to be very stubborn.
S1. I'm willing to try it if it's sensible to do so.
S2. It would be foolish of him not at least to listen.

Conversation B

S1. It's hard to get fast service in this store.
S2. I'm always reluctant to shop here because of that.
S1. I guess it's silly to get angry over such a small thing.
S2. And I'm sure it would be useless to complain to the manager.

Conversation C

S1. It's absurd to suspect Robert of having lied to us.
S2. Yes. He's much too honest to do anything like that.
S1. However, it's essential to find out what happened.
S2. I'm too upset about all this to know what to do.

Conversation D

S1. I'm glad to hear that you've found a good job.
S2. I think I was lucky to find one so quickly.
S1. Now I suppose you're eager to get started.
S2. Yes. It'll be wonderful to work in such nice quarters.

Conversation E

S1. Isn't it rather expensive to live in that part of the city?
S2. Perhaps, but it was impossible for us to find anything else-where.
S1. Of course, it must be convenient to live so close to your office.
S2. Yes. It's practical to live there even if it's expensive.

Exercise 1

1. They heard that. They were happy.

They were happy to hear that.

2. He didn't do it. He was unfit.

He was unfit to do it.

3. We saw it. We were lucky.

We were lucky to see it.

4. I announced it. I was proud.

I was proud to announce it.

5. They got it. They were fortunate.

They were fortunate to get it.

6. She didn't say that. She was reluctant.

She was reluctant to say that.

7. You helped her. You were considerate.

You were considerate to help her.

8. We won it. We were grateful.

We were grateful to win it.

9. I didn't stop them. I was powerless.

I was powerless to stop them.

10. They explored it. They were curious.

They were curious to explore it.

11. You welcomed him. You were discreet.

You were discreet to welcome him.

12. He didn't attempt it. He was afraid.

He was afraid to attempt it.

13. She forgave them. She was glad.

She was glad to forgive them.

14. We explained it. We were ready.

We were ready to explain it.

15. He didn't begin it. He was unable.

He was unable to begin it.

16. They assisted me. They were good.

They were good to assist me.

Exercise 2

1. She'll hear it. She'll be disturbed.

She'll be disturbed to hear it.

2. We know that. We're pleased.

We're pleased to know that.

3. He has them. He's been thrilled.

He's been thrilled to have them.

4. She assisted me. She was contented.

She was contented to assist me.

5. They'll get it. They'll be irritated.

They'll be irritated to get it.

6. I explain that. I'm always rewarded.

I'm always rewarded to explain that.

7. She found it out. She was annoyed.

She was annoyed to find it out.

8. They'll start it. They'll be reassured.

They'll be reassured to start it.

9. He got it across. He was satisfied.

He was satisfied to get it across.

10. She's seen it. She's been impressed.

She's been impressed to see it.

11. We lost them. We were dismayed.

We were dismayed to lose them.

12. I'll study that. I'm very stimulated.

I'm very stimulated to study that.

13. He'll propose that. He'll be prepared.

He'll be prepared to propose that.

14. She began it. She was very excited.

She was very excited to begin it.

15. We collect them. We've been amused.

We've been amused to collect them.

16. They'll use it. They'll be frightened.

They'll be frightened to use it.

Conversation A

S1. Why didn't Peter finish the whole job?
S2. I don't know. He seemed eager to do it.
S1. Maybe he was afraid to show his work to anyone.
S2. Well, I know he was anxious to get started this morning.

Conversation B

S1. How do you like your new job as a receptionist?
S2. Well, it's interesting to meet so many people.
S1. But isn't it boring to say the same things all day long?
S2. Sometimes it gets a little monotonous.

Conversation C

S1. I was thrilled to hear the news.
S2. Your parents will be pleased to hear it too.
S1. Wasn't it exciting to hear that you had won the prize?
S2. Yes, but it was hard to believe.

Conversation D

S1. It was kind of Mary and Alice to help us.
S2. I'm sure they were glad to do it.
S1. We were lucky to have such good assistants, weren't we?
S2. Yes, and it was pleasant to work with them, I thought.

Conversation E

S1. Is Tom willing to go with the visitors tomorrow?
S2. Yes. He said he'd be delighted to do it.
S1. It's nice of him to help us this way.
S2. Yes, it is. We're fortunate to have such a good friend.

Exercise 1

1. She'll be disturbed to hear it.

    It'll disturb her to hear it.

2. We're pleased to know that.

    It pleases us to know that.

3. He's been thrilled to have them.

    It's thrilled him to have them.

4. I was contented to assist her.

    It contented me to assist her.

5. They'll be irritated to get it.

    It'll irritate them to get it.

6. She's rewarded to explain that.

    It rewards her to explain that.

7. I was annoyed to find it out.

    It annoyed me to find it out.

8. They'll be delighted to start it.

    It'll delight them to start it.

9. He was satisfied to get them back.

    It satisfied him to get them back.

10. I was impressed to read it.

    It impressed me to read it.

Exercise 2

1. It annoyed me to find it out.

    Finding it out annoyed me.

2. It'll delight them to start it.

    Starting it will delight them.

3. It satisfied him to get them back.

    Getting them back satisfied him.

4. It's impressed me to read it.

    Reading it has impressed me.

5. It dismayed us to lose them.

    Losing them dismayed us.

6. It'll inspire him to study hard.

    Studying hard will inspire him.

7. It'll interest me to hear about it.

    Hearing about it will interest me.

8. It excited her to receive them.

    Receiving them excited her.

9. It's amused me to collect them.

    Collecting them has amused me.

10. It'll frighten them to use it

    Using it will frighten them.

Exercise 3

1. He thanked them. He was polite.

It was polite of him to thank them.

2. He didn't thank them. He was rude.

It was rude of him not to thank them.

3. He spent his money. He was foolish.

It was foolish of him to spend his money.

4. He didn't spend his money. He was wise.

It was wise of him not to spend his money.

5. He locked the door. He was cautious.

It was cautious of him to lock the door.

6. He didn't lock the door. He was careless.

It was careless of him not to lock the door.

7. He shared the food. He was generous.

It was generous of him to share the food.

8. He didn't share the food. He was selfish.

It was selfish of him not to share the food.

9. He helped us. He was good.

It was good of him to help us.

10. He didn't tell them. He was dishonest.

It was dishonest of him not to tell them.

11. He answered truthfully. He was sensible.

It was sensible of him to answer truthfully.

12. He offered us a ride. He was considerate.

It was considerate of him to offer us a ride.

13. He didn't say anything. He was discreet.

It was discreet of him not to say anything.

14. He did it that way. He was clever.

It was clever of him to do it that way.

15. He didn't complain at all. He was kind.

It was kind of him not to complain at all.

16. He invited us to go. He was thoughtful.

It was thoughtful of him to invite us to go.

Conversation A

S1.   This food is too hot to eat.
S2.   Be careful. It's hot enough to burn your tongue.
S1.   It will be cool enough to eat if we wait a few minutes.
S2.   Yes, but let's not wait until it's too cool to enjoy.

Conversation B

S1.   The man's explanation was too complicated to understand.
S2.   He doesn't speak slowly enough for us to take notes either.
S1.   He gets too excited to remember us students, I think.
S2.   Are you brave enough to ask him to repeat everything?

Conversation C

S1.   The wind is really strong today.
S2.   I'm afraid it's too strong for us to consider going sailing.
S1.   Definitely. It's blowing hard enough to tip a boat over.
S2.   Maybe it will get calm enough later for us to go out.

Conversation D

S1.   I couldn't finish all the work this afternoon.
S2.   It was really too much to finish in one day.
S1.   To tell the truth, there was enough work to keep me busy two days.
S2.   But you're experienced enough to do it faster than anyone else.

Conversation E

S1.   Why doesn't the company try this new method of production?
S2.   The new method is too dangerous to be considered.
S1.   Then will the company continue to use the old method?
S2.   Yes. The old method is still safe enough to be used.

Exercise 1

1. He didn't finish it. He was very nervous.

   He was too nervous to finish it.

2. I didn't hear that. I was very confused.

   I was too confused to hear that.

3. We didn't say anything. We were very angry.

   We were too angry to say anything.

4. They didn't do it. They were very discouraged.

   They were too discouraged to do it.

5. She didn't read that. She was very busy then.

   She was too busy then to read that.

6. I didn't meet them there. I was very lazy.

   I was too lazy to meet them there.

7. They didn't help us. They were very insulted.

   They were too insulted to help us.

8. She didn't return that. She was very upset.

   She was too upset to return that.

9. We didn't describe it well. We were very excited.

   We were too excited to describe it well.

10. I didn't prepare for it at all. I was very annoyed.

    I was too annoyed to prepare for it at all.

11. She didn't speak about it. She was very ashamed.

    She was too ashamed to speak about it.

12. They didn't keep it up. They were very tired by that time.

    They were too tired by that time to keep it up.

13. He didn't send for them. He was very discreet.

    He was too discreet to send for them.

14. We didn't bring it up at the meeting. We were very depressed.

    We were too depressed to bring it up at the meeting.

15. They didn't begin the work. They were very afraid.

    They were too afraid to begin the work.

16. I didn't turn the offer down. I was very interested.

    I was too interested to turn the offer down.

Exercise 2

1. The food was very hot. I couldn't eat it.

   The food was too hot for me to eat.

2. The food was very hot. It burned my tongue.

   The food was hot enough to burn my tongue.

3. The suit is dirty. You can't wear it tomorrow.

   The suit is too dirty for you to wear tomorrow.

4. The suit is clean. You can wear it tomorrow.

   The suit is clean enough for you to wear tomorrow.

5. The water is very cold now. You can't go swimming.

   The water is too cold now for you to go swimming.

6. The water is quite warm now. You can go swimming.

   The water is warm enough now for you to go swimming.

7. The rope was very long. It reached to the bottom.

   The rope was long enough to reach to the bottom.

8. The rope wasn't very long. It didn't reach to the bottom.

   The rope wasn't long enough to reach to the bottom.

9. The rope was very short. It didn't reach to the bottom.

   The rope was too short to reach to the bottom.

10. I'm quite strong. I can lift that box without help.

    I'm strong enough to lift that box without help.

11. I'm quite weak. I can't lift that box without help.

    I'm too weak to lift that box without help.

12. He's very bright. He can solve the problem by himself.

    He's bright enough to solve the problem by himself.

13. He's upset now. He can't talk about the problem.

    He's too upset now to talk about the problem.

14. The work was very hard. We weren't able to finish it.

    The work was too hard for us to finish.

15. That method is dangerous. It can't be considered.

    That method is too dangerous to be considered.

16. The other method is quite safe. It can be used.

    The other method is safe enough to be used.

Conversation A

S1. Whom is Mary talking to?
S2. She's talking to her cousin.
S1. What's she talking about?
S2. She's talking about her new job.

Conversation B

S1. What are Tom and Fred arguing about?
S2. They're arguing about politics.
S1. What's Tom objecting to?
S2. He's objecting to some of Fred's statements.

Conversation C

S1. What part of the lesson did you have trouble with?
S2. I had trouble with several parts.
S1. Whom did you explain your problems to?
S2. I explained them to Mr. Taylor.

Conversation D

S1. What does Tom devote his spare time to.
S2. He devotes most of it to his hobbies.
S1. What does he concentrate on mostly?
S2. On photography, I think.

Conversation E

S1. Whom does that woman remind you of?
S2. Is it somebody I work with?
S1. No. Somebody you're very friendly with.
S2. Now I know. You mean Mary Wilson.

Exercise 1

1.	He benefited from that.	What did he benefit from?
2.	They'll concentrate on that.	What will they concentrate on?
3.	I should insist on that.	What should you insist on?
4.	She contributes to that.	What does she contribute to?
5.	He can succeed in that.	What can he succeed in?
6.	I suffered from that.	What did you suffer from?
7.	They must believe in that.	What must they believe in?
8.	She's prepared for that.	What's she prepared for?
9.	I recovered from that.	What did you recover from?
10.	They'll object to that.	What will they object to?
11.	John can comment on that.	What can he comment on?
12.	I wondered about that.	What did you wonder about?
13.	She must consent to that.	What must she consent to?
14.	They've qualified for that.	What have they qualified for?
15.	He'll worry about that.	What will he worry about?
16.	They're quarreling over that.	What are they quarreling over?

Exercise 2

1.	Has she been invited?	What's she been invited to?
2.	Weren't you convinced?	What weren't you convinced of?
3.	Will they be respected?	What will they be respected for?
4.	Couldn't he be assured?	What couldn't he be assured of?
5.	Must you be prepared?	What must you be prepared for?
6.	Was he convicted?	What was he convicted of?
7.	Haven't you been pleased?	What haven't you been pleased with?
8.	Should she be rewarded?	What should she be rewarded for?
9.	Are they committed?	What are they committed to?
10.	Will you be opposed?	What will you be opposed to?

11. Was he reprimanded?   What was he reprimanded for?

12. Are they appreciated?   What are they appreciated for?

13. Has Mary been devoted?   What has Mary been devoted to?

14. Should I be ashamed?   What should I be ashamed of?

15. Must we be acquainted?   What must we be acquainted with?

16. Could they be accused?   What could they be accused of?

Conversation A

S1.   What did they complain about?
S2   They complained about all the noise.
S1.   Whom did you refer them to?
S2.   I referred them to the manager.

Conversation B

S1.   What are you upset about?
S2.   About the things you said.
S1.   Is it something I should apologize for?
S2.   It certainly is.

Conversation C

S1.   Whom did you get the information from?
S2.   From my friend Robert.
S1.   Is he a person you can rely on to be accurate?
S2.   That's something I'm very sure of.

Conversation D

S1.   Whom were you quarreling with?
S2.   I was quarreling with another student.
S1.   What were you quarreling with him about?
S2.   About the coming election.

Conversation E

S1.   Whom did Mary disagree with?
S2.   She disagreed with Mr. Black.
S1.   What did she disagree with him on?
S2.   On the subject of foreign relations.

Exercise 1

1. It detracted.	What did it detract from?
2. It must correspond.	What must it correspond to?
3. It provides.	What does it provide for?
4. It'll agree.	What will it agree with?
5. It has to conform.	What does it have to conform to?
6. It was combined.	What was it combined with?
7. It's interfering.	What's it interfering with?
8. It should contribute.	What should it contribute to?
9. It'll contrast.	What will it contrast with?
10. It applies.	What does it apply to?
11. It's conflicted.	What has it conflicted with?
12. It differed.	What did it differ from?
13. It must correlate.	What must it correlate with?
14. It'll relate.	What will it relate to?
15. It all depends.	What does it all depend on?
16. It can compensate.	What can it compensate for?

Exercise 2

1. He'll apologize to them.	Whom will he apologize to?
2. He'll apologize for that.	What will he apologize for?
3. She quarreled with him.	Whom did she quarrel with?
4. They quarreled about that.	What did they quarrel about?
5. He can apply to them.	Whom can he apply to?
6. He can apply for that.	What can he apply for?
7. They agree with her.	Whom do they agree with?
8. They agree on that.	What do they agree on?
9. He's arguing with them.	Who's he arguing with?
10. He's arguing about that.	What's he arguing about?
11. She can complain to him.	Whom can she complain to?
12. She can complain about that.	What can she complain about?
13. They spoke to him.	Whom did they speak to?
14. They spoke about that.	What did they speak about?
15. He lied to her.	Whom did he lie to?
16. He lied about that.	What did he lie about?

Conversation A

S1. Were you quarreling with John about something?
S2. No. We were just talking about the political situation.
S1. Does John's opinion differ greatly from yours?
S2. Not much. We agree on almost everything.

Conversation B

S1. Are you worrying about something?
S2. Yes. My job is interfering with my studies.
S1. Why do you insist on studying and working at the same time?
S2. I want to finish school, but I also need money.

Conversation C

S1. Have you inquired about their reasons for staying?
S2. No, because I don't think they would confide in me.
S1. If you associate with them more, maybe they will.
S2. Possibly, but I doubt it.

Conversation D

S1. Are you going to comment on the new regulation?
S2. Yes. I think everyone will benefit from my comments.
S1. Do you object to the regulation or approve of it?
S2. Actually, I have mixed feelings about it.

Conversation E

S1. Do you think Tom will succeed in solving the problem?
S2. It depends on a number of things.
S1. I suppose he'll rely on getting a little help from friends.
S2. Yes, and he'll probably confer with Professor Smith too.

Exercise 1

1.	They don't approve of him.	Why don't they approve of him?
2.	I complained to them.	Why did you complain to them?
3.	He can't compete with them.	Why can't he compete with them?
4.	I've worried about him.	Why have you worried about him?
5.	He didn't cooperate with me.	Why didn't he cooperate with you?
6.	We disagreed with her.	Why did you disagree with her?
7.	I have to listen to them.	Why do you have to listen to them?
8.	He hasn't inquired about us.	Why hasn't he inquired about you?
9.	She apologized to them.	Why did she apologize to them?
10.	You should associate with her.	Why should I associate with her?
11.	She confides in him.	Why does she confide in him?
12.	He didn't converse with them.	Why didn't he converse with them?

Exercise 2

Why did he worry about them?

listen	Why did he listen to them?
disagree	Why did he disagree with them?
confide	Why did he confide in them?
inquire	Why did he inquire about them?
converse	Why did he converse with them?
approve	Why did he approve of them?
associate	Why did he associate with them?
complain	Why did he complain to them?
cooperate	Why did he cooperate with them?
compete	Why did he compete with them?
apologize	Why did he apologize to them?
worry	Why did he worry about them?

Exercise 3

1.	Did he benefit from that?	Yes. He benefited from that.
2.	Will they concentrate on that?	Yes. They'll concentrate on that.
3.	Shouldn't you insist on that?	Yes. I should insist on that.
4.	Doesn't she contribute to that?	Yes. She contributes to that.
5.	Can he succeed in that?	Yes. He can succeed in that.
6.	Didn't you quarrel about that?	Yes. We quarreled about that.
7.	Have you applied for that?	Yes. I've applied for that.
8.	Do they believe in that?	Yes. They believe in that.
9.	Won't he complain about that?	Yes. He'll complain about that.
10.	Have you prepared for that?	Yes. I've prepared for that.
11.	Should she apologize for that?	Yes. She should apologize for that.
12.	Don't you wonder about that?	Yes. I wonder about that.
13.	Will they object to that?	Yes. They'll object to that.
14.	Did she recover from that?	Yes. She recovered from that.

Exercise 4

1.	They quarreled.	They quarreled about that.
2.	They objected.	They objected to that.
3.	They succeeded.	They succeeded in that.
4.	They apologized.	They apologized for that.
5.	They benefited.	They benefited from that.
6.	They wondered.	They wondered about that.
7.	They insisted.	They insisted on that.
8.	They applied.	They applied for that.
9.	They recovered.	They recovered from that.
10.	They concentrated.	They concentrated on that.
11.	They contributed.	They contributed to that.
12.	They prepared.	They prepared for that.
13.	They complained.	They complained about that.
14.	They believed.	They believed in that.

Exercise 5

1.	He referred to that.	Why did he refer to that?
2.	I've provided for that.	Why have you provided for that?
3.	They can't rely on that.	Why can't they rely on that?
4.	She disapproves of that.	Why does she disapprove of that?
5.	You must hope for that.	Why must I hope for that?
6.	They won't speak about that.	Why won't they speak about that?
7.	She's depending on that.	Why is she depending on that?
8.	He lied about that.	Why did he lie about that?
9.	You should invest in that.	Why should I invest in that?
10.	I've specialized in that.	Why have you specialized in that?
11.	They didn't search for that.	Why didn't they search for that?
12.	I participated in that.	Why did you participate in that?
13.	He's arguing about that.	Why is he arguing about that?
14.	She's disposed of that.	Why has she disposed of that?

Exercise 6

Why did they speak about that?

rely	Why did they rely on that?
invest	Why did they invest in that?
lie	Why did they lie about that?
depend	Why did they depend on that?
hope	Why did they hope for that?
specialize	Why did they specialize in that?
disapprove	Why did they disapprove of that?
argue	Why did they argue about that?
participate	Why did they participate in that?
dispose	Why did they dispose of that?
search	Why did they search for that?
refer	Why did they refer to that?
provide	Why did they provide for that?

Conversation A

S1.   Did you explain our reasons for going to Mr. White?
S2.   Yes. I explained everything to him.
S1.   Did he question you about anything?
S2.   No, but he reminded me of several things we should do.

Conversation B

S1.   Why is Mary angry at you?
S2.   Well, she blames me for the trouble she's having.
S1.   But you warned her about the possibilities some time ago.
S2.   Yes, and I emphasized that to her.

Conversation C

S1.   Did you consult a lawyer about your tax problems?
S2.   Yes, but he referred me to someone else.
S1.   Whom did he refer you to?
S2.   A lawyer who specializes in tax problems.

Conversation D

S1.   I understand you assisted the girls with their article.
S2.   I just advised them in one or two matters.
S1.   It was very kind of you to help them with it.
S2.   Actually, I devoted very little time to it.

Conversation E

S1.   What did Tom do with the money he won in the contest?
S2.   He donated some of it to charity.
S1.   Did he deposit any in his bank account?
S2.   Yes, and he invested the rest in his brother's business.

Exercise 1

1.	Did she consult him about that?	Yes. She consulted him about that.
2.	Can they accuse you of that?	Yes. They can accuse me of that.
3.	Has he thanked them for that?	Yes. He's thanked them for that.
4.	Do they suspect her of that?	Yes. They suspect her of that.
5.	Will he protect us from that?	Yes. He'll protect us from that.
6.	Can you question her about that?	Yes. I can question her about that.
7.	Did he pay the men for that?	Yes. He paid the men for that.
8.	Should we invite him to that?	Yes. We should invite him to that.
9.	Did he convince her of that?	Yes. He convinced her of that.
10.	Does she respect you for that?	Yes. She respects me for that.
11.	Will they punish him for that?	Yes. They'll punish him for that.
12.	Must she remind them of that?	Yes. She must remind them of that.

Exercise 2

1.	They reminded him.	They reminded him of that.
2.	They invited him.	They invited him to that.
3.	They consulted him.	They consulted him about that.
4.	They paid him.	They paid him for that.
5.	They encouraged him.	They encouraged him in that.
6.	They accused him.	They accused him of that.
7.	They thanked him.	They thanked him for that.
8.	They convinced him.	They convinced him of that.
9.	They punished him.	They punished him for that.
10.	They respected him.	They respected him for that.
11.	They protected him.	They protected him from that.
12.	They questioned him.	They questioned him about that.

Exercise 3

1.	Can you increase it to that?	Yes. I can increase it to that.
2.	Will he identify it as that?	Yes. He'll identify it as that.
3.	Did you deduct it from that?	Yes. I deducted it from that.
4.	Can they omit it from that?	Yes. They can omit it from that.
5.	Has she invested it in that?	Yes. She's invested it in that.
6.	Can he replace it with that?	Yes. He can replace it with that.
7.	Should we add it to that?	Yes. You should add it to that.
8.	Do they derive it from that?	Yes. They derive it from that.
9.	Is he combining it with that?	Yes. He's combining it with that.
10.	Has Mary related it to that?	Yes. Mary has related it to that.
11.	Will they donate it to that?	Yes. They'll donate it to that.
12.	Can we accompany it with that?	Yes. You can accompany it with that.
13.	Did she exchange it for that?	Yes. She exchanged it for that.
14.	Will they confine it to that?	Yes. They'll confine it to that.

Exercise 4

1.	We exchanged it.	We exchanged it for that.
2.	We omitted it.	We omitted it from that.
3.	We donated it.	We donated it to that.
4.	We identified it.	We identified it as that.
5.	We increased it.	We increased it to that.
6.	We confined it.	We confined it to that.
7.	We deducted it.	We deducted it from that.
8.	We accompanied it.	We accompanied it with that.
9.	We invested it.	We invested it in that.
10.	We related it.	We related it to that.
11.	We replaced it.	We replaced it with that.
12.	We derived it.	We derived it from that.
13.	We combined it.	We combined it with that.
14.	We added it.	We added it to that.

Exercise 5

1. Will they blame you for that?

Yes. They'll blame me for that.

2. Did he notify them of that?

Yes. He notified them of that.

3. Can she provide him with that?

Yes. She can provide him with that.

4. Do you envy him for that?

Yes. I envy him for that.

5. Did they tease her about that?

Yes. They teased her about that.

6. Can he supply you with that?

Yes. He can supply me with that.

7. Does he admire them for that?

Yes. He admires them for that.

8. Can they direct him to that?

Yes. They can direct him to that.

9. Will he excuse them from that?

Yes. He'll excuse them from that.

10. Has she warned you about that?

Yes. She's warned me about that.

11. Did he compensate you for that?

Yes. He compensated me for that.

12. Did they force him into that?

Yes. They forced him into that.

13. Will she forgive him for that?

Yes. She'll forgive him for that.

Exercise 6

1. He warned them.   He warned them about that.
2. He notified them.   He notified them of that.
3. He forced them.   He forced them into that.
4. He blamed them.   He blamed them for that.
5. He forgave them.   He forgave them for that.
6. He provided them.   He provided them with that.
7. He envied them.   He envied them for that.
8. He teased them.   He teased them about that.
9. He excused them.   He excused them from that.
10. He warned them.   He warned them about that.
11. He compensated them.   He compensated them for that.
12. He supplied them.   He supplied them with that.
13. He directed them.   He directed them to that.

Conversation Drill A

S1. I saw them about that yesterday.
S2. Did they ___(A)___ you _____ it?
S1. Well, they ___(B)___ it.
S2. I suppose that was to be expected.

(A)	(B)
blame . . . for	complained about
warn . . . about	worried about
advise . . . of	commented on
encourage . . . in	inquired about
remind . . . of	referred to
question . . . about	spoke about
pay . . . for	consented to
assist . . . with	argued about

Conversation Drill B

S1. He's going to see them tomorrow.
S2. Do you think he'll ___(A)___ them _____ that?
S1. He certainly ought to ___(B)___ it _____ them.
S2. At any rate, he has to do something.

(A)	(B)
consult . . . about	explain . . . to
threaten . . . with	suggest . . . to
caution . . . about	emphasize . . . to
furnish . . . with	divide . . . among
excuse . . . from	require . . . of
provide . . . with	share . . . with
trust . . . with	offer . . . to
advise . . . of	conceal . . . from

Conversation A

S1. Smith is very popular with his employees, isn't he?

S2. Yes, he is. He's always been very fair to them.

S1. I know he always seems to be aware of other people's problems.

S2. I think that's why he's been so successful in his work.

Conversation B

S1. How do you like your new teacher?

S2. Very well. He's always patient with us.

S1. Doesn't he ever get angry with his students?

S2. No. He never seems to get upset over anything.

Conversation C

S1. My secretary is very efficient in everything she does.

S2. You're lucky. Secretaries aren't always careful about their work.

S1. Right. My former secretary was often neglectful of things.

S2. Well, I advise you to be very courteous to your new one.

Conversation D

S1. Are you optimistic about the results of the examination?

S2. To be truthful about it, I'm really not.

S1. I'm not very confident of getting a good grade either.

S2. I guess it's no use to be so anxious about it now.

Conversation E

S1. My boss has been critical of my work lately.

S2. Has your recent work been consistent with your previous work?

S1. If anything, I'd say it's been superior to my previous work.

S2. Then maybe he's resentful of you for some other reason.

Exercise 1

1. He was afraid, wasn't he?

   Yes. He was afraid of the man.

2. She's often rude, isn't she?

   Yes. She's often rude to the man.

3. They won't be patient, will they?

   No. They won't be patient with the man.

4. You've been angry, haven't you?

   Yes. I've been angry with the man.

5. He was antagonistic, wasn't he?

   Yes. He was antagonistic toward the man.

6. I haven't been courteous, have I?

   No. You haven't been courteous to the man.

7. She used to be hostile, didn't she?

   Yes. She used to be hostile toward the man.

8. They're always loyal, aren't they?

   Yes. They're always loyal to the man.

9. You'll be friendly, won't you?

   Yes. I'll be friendly to the man.

10. John was good, wasn't he?

    Yes. John was good to the man.

11. You shouldn't be jealous, should you?

    No. I shouldn't be jealous of the man.

12. He isn't very intimate, is he?

    No. He isn't very intimate with the man.

13. She won't be envious, will she?

    No. She won't be envious of the man.

14. They were considerate, weren't they?

    Yes. They were considerate of the man.

15. He wouldn't be cruel, would he?

    No. He wouldn't be cruel to the man.

16. They're all proud, aren't they?

    Yes. They're all proud of the man.

17. She was always resentful, wasn't she?

    Yes. She was always resentful of the man.

18. He's been quite truthful, hasn't he?

    Yes. He's been quite truthful with the man.

19. They won't be critical, will they?

    No. They won't be critical of the man.

Exercise 2

1.	Wasn't he optimistic?	Yes. He was optimistic about that.
2.	Are they all proficient?	Yes. They're all proficient in that.
3.	Have you been aware?	Yes. I've been aware of that.
4.	Won't she be fearful?	Yes. She'll be fearful of that.
5.	Is he really contemptuous?	Yes. He's really contemptuous of that.
6.	Haven't you been pessimistic?	Yes. I've been pessimistic about that.
7.	Are they all innocent?	Yes. They're all innocent of that.
8.	Will some be intolerant?	Yes. Some will be intolerant of that.
9.	Were you impatient?	Yes. I was impatient about that.
10.	Wasn't the boy sorry?	Yes. The boy was sorry about that.
11.	Can't they be responsible?	Yes. They can be responsible for that.
12.	Should the man be earnest?	Yes. The man should be earnest about that.
13.	Were the men intent?	Yes. The men were intent on that.
14.	Must you be skillful?	Yes. I must be skillful at that.
15.	Wasn't she upset?	Yes. She was upset over that.
16.	Aren't you all envious?	Yes. We're all envious of that.

Conversation Drill A

S1. What did the men say about the new secretary?
S2. Apparently, she's ___(A)___ working hard.
S1. In your opinion, is she ___(B)___ the things she must do?
S2. I would certainly say she is.

(A)	(B)
capable of	skillful at
fond of	proficient in
not afraid of	suitable for
desirous of	efficient in
intent on	careful about
not resentful of	adequate for
amenable to	aware of
not critical of	familiar with

Conversation Drill B

S1. What's your opinion of our new president?
S2. I like him because he's ___(A)___ other people.
S1. He's certainly ___(B)___ everyone.
S2. Obviously, he's a fine person for the job.

(A)	(B)
always considerate of	polite to
never critical of	gentle with
always kind to	friendly toward
never rude to	cooperative with
always patient with	acceptable to
never envious of	thoughtful of
always respectful of	popular with
never hostile toward	truthful with
always courteous to	trustful of
never unfair to	generous with

Conversation A

S1. What sports are you interested in?
S2. Well, I get quite excited about football.
S1. Do you get absorbed in games on TV, as my brother does?
S2. I'm afraid I do. Almost every weekend.

Conversation B

S1. Is something the matter?
S2. Well, I'm concerned about my job.
S1. Is it related to all the recent changes?
S2. Yes. I'm having trouble getting adjusted to my new duties.

Conversation C

S1. Are you accustomed to the climate here yet?
S2. Not really. I get tired of the constant rain.
S1. You certainly can't be blamed for that.
S2. I'll really be glad when the spring comes.

Conversation D

S1. Are you acquainted with that man over there?
S2. Yes. I'm associated with him in my work.
S1. I enjoyed talking to him very much.
S2. I'm not surprised at that. He's very charming.

Conversation E

S1. Did you get involved in the argument at the meeting?
S2. Yes. I didn't want to be accused of not having an opinion.
S1. I got very annoyed over several things that Harold said.
S2. To tell the truth, I was very disappointed in him.

Exercise 1

1.	Will they be tired of that?	Yes. They'll be tired of that.
2.	Aren't you accustomed to that?	Yes. I'm accustomed to that.
3.	Should we be satisfied with that?	Yes. You should be satisfied with that.
4.	Hasn't he been reminded of that?	Yes. He's been reminded of that.
5.	Must she be concerned about that?	Yes. She must be concerned about that.
6.	Haven't you been influenced by that?	Yes. I've been influenced by that.
7.	Can they be blamed for that?	Yes. They can be blamed for that.
8.	Wasn't she notified of that?	Yes. She was notified of that.
9.	Will they be excited about that?	Yes. They'll be excited about that.
10.	Should he be involved in that?	Yes. He should be involved in that.
11.	Were they deprived of that?	Yes. They were deprived of that.
12.	Aren't you interested in that?	Yes. I'm interested in that.
13.	Will she be impressed by that?	Yes. She'll be impressed by that.
14.	Should I be offended by that?	Yes. You should be offended by that.
15.	Weren't you prepared for that?	Yes. I was prepared for that.
16.	Are they displeased with that?	Yes. They're displeased with that.

Exercise 2

1.	Will they be tired?	Why will they be tired of that?
2.	Aren't you accustomed?	Why aren't you accustomed to that?
3.	Should we be satisfied?	Why should we be satisfied with that?

4. Hasn't he been reminded? / Why hasn't he been reminded of that?

5. Must she be concerned? / Why must she be concerned about that?

6. Haven't you been influenced? / Why haven't you been influenced by that?

7. Can they be blamed? / Why can they be blamed for that?

8. Wasn't she notified? / Why wasn't she notified of that?

9. Will they be excited? / Why will they be excited about that?

10. Should he be involved? / Why should he be involved in that?

11. Were they deprived? / Why were they deprived of that?

12. Aren't you interested? / Why aren't you interested in that?

13. Will she be impressed? / Why will she be impressed by that?

14. Should I be offended? / Why should I be offended by that?

15. Weren't you prepared? / Why weren't you prepared for that?

16. Are they displeased? / Why are they displeased with that?

Exercise 3

1. They'll be indebted to the man. / Why will they be indebted to him?

2. Wasn't he devoted to the man? / Why wasn't he devoted to him?

3. I've been influenced by the man. / Why have you been influenced by him?

4. We're all accustomed to the man. / Why are you all accustomed to him?

5. He shouldn't be offended by the man. / Why shouldn't he be offended by him?

6. No one was acquainted with the man. / Why wasn't anyone acquainted with him?

7. They're amazed at the man.

Why are they amazed at him?

8. You must be concerned about the man.

Why must I be concerned about him?

9. We won't be disappointed in the man.

Why won't you be disappointed in him?

10. She used to be interested in the man.

Why did she use to be interested in him?

11. Everyone is disgusted with the man.

Why is everyone disgusted with him?

12. I had to be associated with the man.

Why did you have to be associated with him?

13. You shouldn't be displeased with the man.

Why shouldn't I be displeased with him?

14. Weren't they insulted by the man?

Why were they insulted by him?

15. You mustn't be ashamed of the man.

Why mustn't I be ashamed of him?

16. She's been provoked with the man.

Why has she been provoked with him?

Exercise 4

1. They'll be indebted.

They'll be indebted to the man.

2. Wasn't he devoted?

Wasn't he devoted to the man?

3. I've been influenced.

I've been influenced by the man.

4. We're all accustomed.

We're all accustomed to the man.

5. He shouldn't be offended.

He shouldn't be offended by the man.

6. No one was acquainted.

No one was acquainted with the man.

7. Are they related?

Are they related to the man?

8. You mustn't be concerned.

You mustn't be concerned about the man.

9. We won't be disappointed.

We won't be disappointed in the man.

10.	She used to be interested.	She used to be interested in the man.
11.	Everyone is disgusted.	Everyone is disgusted with the man.
12.	I had to be associated.	I had to be associated with the man.
13.	Don't be displeased.	Don't be displeased with the man.
14.	Weren't they insulted?	Weren't they insulted by the man?
15.	You shouldn't be ashamed.	You shouldn't be ashamed of the man.
16.	She's been provoked.	She's been provoked with the man.

Conversation A

S1.   Tom seemed to become nervous when he noticed the time.
S2.   He spoke nervously too, I thought.
S1.   I noticed he made a quick departure afterward.
S2.   Yes. He did leave rather quickly, didn't he?

Conversation B

S1.   Is the director a well-educated man?
S2.   Yes. He has a good education.
S1.   Is he a very efficient person on the job?
S2.   Yes, he is. He always seems to do things efficiently.

Conversation C

S1.   Was the man angry?
S2.   Yes. He shouted at us very angrily.
S1.   Were people calm about it or not?
S2.   Most of us took it quite calmly.

Conversation D

S1.   Helen is a calm person.
S2.   I've noticed she always speaks calmly.
S1.   She also seems sensible about things.
S2.   Yes. She always handles things sensibly, in my opinion.

Conversation E

S1.   Mr. White looked anxious, don't you think?
S2.   Yes. He was pacing the floor anxiously when I saw him.
S1.   Is he always so emotional about making speeches?
S2.   Yes. He gets very involved emotionally.

Exercise 1

1. He made rapid movements. | He made movements rapidly.
2. He used the correct expression. | He used the expression correctly.
3. He made a sudden comment. | He made a comment suddenly.
4. He asked respectful questions. | He asked questions respectfully.
5. He made precise gestures. | He made gestures precisely.
6. He wrote very careful reports. | He wrote reports very carefully.
7. He made a dramatic statement. | He made a statement dramatically.
8. He expressed his sincere emotions. | He expressed his emotions sincerely.
9. He told extremely humorous jokes. | He told jokes extremely humorously.
10. He wrote frequent descriptions. | He wrote descriptions frequently.
11. He told amusing stories. | He told stories amusingly.
12. He gave us quite accurate information. | He gave us information quite accurately.
13. He told her his honest opinion. | He told her his opinion honestly.
14. He made several hasty calls. | He made several calls hastily.
15. He demanded an immediate apology. | He demanded an apology immediately.
16. He asked us rather clever questions. | He asked us questions rather cleverly.

Exercise 2

1. She's very modest. | She speaks very modestly.
2. They were resentful. | They spoke resentfully.
3. You haven't been nervous. | You haven't spoken nervously.
4. Everyone will be considerate. | Everyone will speak considerately.
5. We won't be skeptical. | We won't speak skeptically.

6. She was just being fair.

She was just speaking fairly.

7. You should be brave.

You should speak bravely.

8. We have to be practical.

We have to speak practically.

9. I'm always sympathetic.

I always speak sympathetically.

10. John is being very quiet.

John is speaking very quietly.

11. They could have been polite.

They could have spoken politely.

12. You must be interesting.

You must speak interestingly.

13. Please try to be sensible.

Please try to speak sensibly.

14. I should have been suspicious.

I should have spoken suspiciously.

15. She wasn't really critical.

She didn't really speak critically.

16. He used to be enthusiastic.

He used to speak enthusiastically.

Conversation A

S1. Does Peter always speak rapidly?
S2. Usually, but not when he makes speeches.
S1. He's a good speaker, and his pronunciation is excellent.
S2. He does pronounce words well, doesn't he?

Conversation B

S1. Was the president completely satisfied with the results?
S2. Yes, he was. He expressed complete satisfaction.
S1. Did he announce the results of our work formally?
S2. Yes, he did. He made a formal announcement.

Conversation C

S1. Did you consider everything impartially?
S2. Yes. I tried to give everything very impartial consideration.
S1. You treated the matter cautiously, I see.
S2. Well, it definitely called for cautious treatment.

Conversation D

S1. Did the chairman make a recommendation to oppose changes?
S2. Yes, and he recommended opposition to the new proposal.
S1. Was there any criticism of the proposal?
S2. Yes. Some people criticized it and proposed further study.

Conversation E

S1. The boys behaved badly and deserved punishment.
S2. After the party, their parents punished them for their bad behavior.
S1. Did they apologize for their rude remarks?
S2. Yes. They made an apology for having spoken so rudely.

Exercise 1 / Line A1 /

Does Peter always speak rapidly?

work	Does Peter always work rapidly?
carefully	Does Peter always work carefully?
usually	Does Peter usually work carefully?
write	Does Peter usually write carefully?
accurately	Does Peter usually write accurately?

Exercise 2 / Lines A1 and A3 /

Peter is a rapid speaker.

worker	Peter is a rapid worker.
careful	Peter is a careful worker.
the boys	The boys are careful workers.
good writers	The boys are good writers.
accurate	The boys are accurate writers.

Exercise 3 / Line B4 /

He made a formal announcement.

recommendation	He made a formal recommendation.
immediate	He made an immediate recommendation.
suggestion	He made an immediate suggestion.
cautious	He made a cautious suggestion.
reference	He made a cautious reference.

Exercise 4 / Line C3 /

You treated the matter with caution.

tact	You treated the matter with tact.
handled	You handled the matter with tact.
care	You handled the matter with care.
discussed	You discussed the matter with care.

Exercise 5 / Line C4 /

It definitely called for cautious treatment.

tactful	It definitely called for tactful treatment.
handling	It definitely called for tactful handling.
careful	It definitely called for careful handling.
discussion	It definitely called for careful discussion.

Exercise 6

1. They're rapid translators.   They translate rapidly.
2. He's a dramatic speaker.   He speaks dramatically.
3. She's a careful listener.   She listens carefully.
4. We're loyal followers.   We follow loyally.
5. You two are steady workers.   You two work steadily.
6. They're cautious planners.   They plan cautiously.
7. I'm a terrible speller.   I spell terribly.
8. You're humorous speakers.   You speak humorously.
9. You're an accurate writer.   You write accurately.
10. You're both wise shoppers.   You both shop wisely.
11. She's a regular helper.   She helps regularly.
12. I'm a clumsy dancer.   I dance clumsily.
13. They're energetic teachers.   They teach energetically.
14. We're attentive listeners.   We listen attentively.
15. You're a sincere speaker.   You speak sincerely.
16. He's an efficient supervisor.   He supervises efficiently.

Exercise 7

1. They'll speak considerately.   They'll be considerate.
2. I won't speak skeptically.   I won't be skeptical.
3. She speaks very modestly.   She's very modest.
4. She was just speaking fairly.   She was just being fair.
5. They spoke resentfully.   They were resentful.
6. You haven't spoken nervously.   You haven't been nervous.
7. Someone must speak bravely.   Someone must be brave.
8. We have to speak practically.   We have to be practical.
9. I always speak sympathetically.   I'm always sympathetic.
10. John is speaking very quietly.   John is being very quiet.
11. They could have spoken politely.   They could have been polite.
12. You should speak humorously.   You should be humorous.

13. Please try to speak sensibly.   Please try to be sensible.
14. They've spoken suspiciously.   They've been suspicious.
15. She didn't speak critically.   She wasn't critical.
16. He used to speak enthusiastically. He used to be enthusiastic.

Exercise 8

1. He announced it.   His announcement interested people.
2. We considered it.   Our consideration interested people.
3. I recommended it.   My recommendation interested people.
4. They opposed it.   Their opposition interested people.
5. She criticized it.   Her criticism interested people.
6. We proposed it.   Our proposal interested people.
7. They explained it.   Their explanation interested people.
8. I described it.   My description interested people.
9. He improved it.   His improvement interested people.
10. They discovered it.   Their discovery interested people.
11. She discussed it.   Her discussion interested people.
12. I examined it.   My examination interested people.
13. They suspected it.   Their suspicion interested people.
14. He defended it.   His defense interested people.
15. We denied it.   Our denial interested people.
16. They predicted it.   Their prediction interested people.

Exercise 9

1. He relied on them.   His reliance on them was important.
2. He prepared for that.   His preparation for that was important.
3. He invested in that.   His investment in that was important.
4. He competed with them.   His competition with them was important.
5. He protested about that. His protest about that was important.
6. He succeeded in that.   His success in that was important.

7. He provided for that.

His provision for that was important.

8. He replied to them.

His reply to them was important.

9. He participated in that.

His participation in that was important.

10. He cooperated with them.

His cooperation with them was important.

11. He recovered from that.

His recovery from that was important.

12. He persisted in that.

His persistence in that was important.

13. He depended on them.

His dependence on them was important.

14. He referred to that.

His referral to that was important.

15. He disagreed with them.

His disagreement with them was important.

16. He speculated on that.

His speculation on that was important.

Conversation A

S1. I tried to instruct John how to get there.
S2. Did he understand your instructions? .
S1. Well, I described every place along the way in detail.
S2. Then I'm sure your description made everything clear.

Conversation B

S1. Did you see the demonstration of that new product?
S2. Yes, but it was demonstrated in a different building.
S1. Did the quick change in plans confuse people?
S2. Fortunately, there seemed to be very little confusion.

Conversation C

S1. Robert decided not to say anything about his good luck.
S2. I think he made a wise decision. Don't you?
S1. Definitely. I admire him for it too.
S2. Without question, he deserves a great deal of admiration.

Conversation D

S1. We just recently agreed on a course of action.
S2. What brought about this agreement?
S1. We investigated and then concluded it was necessary.
S2. I came to the same conclusion after some investigation.

Conversation E

S1. My friend selected everything he needed very quickly.
S2. But his selections were quite good, I thought.
S1. How could he choose things so quickly?
S2. I don't know, but his choices were all very good.

Exercise 1

1.	They admired him.	Their admiration was apparent.
2.	We suspected them.	Our suspicion was apparent.
3.	She trusted us.	Her trust was apparent.
4.	They encouraged him.	Their encouragement was apparent.
5.	We guided them.	Our guidance was apparent.
6.	He persuaded us.	His persuasion was apparent.
7.	They recommended her.	Their recommendation was apparent.
8.	She supported them.	Her support was apparent.
9.	He advised them.	His advice was apparent.
10.	We offended him.	Our offense was apparent.
11.	She flattered them.	Her flattery was apparent.
12.	I reassured him.	My reassurance was apparent.
13.	He instructed her.	His instruction was apparent.
14.	You deceived them.	Your deception was apparent.
15.	They respected him.	Their respect was apparent.
16.	We assisted her.	Our assistance was apparent.

Exercise 2

1.	They approved of that.	I mentioned their approval of that.
2.	They depended on him.	I mentioned their dependence on him.
3.	They contributed to that.	I mentioned their contribution to that.
4.	They applied for that.	I mentioned their application for that.
5.	They apologized to him.	I mentioned their apology to him.
6.	They insisted on that.	I mentioned their insistence on that.
7.	They complained to him.	I mentioned their complaint to him.
8.	They inquired about that.	I mentioned their inquiry about that.
9.	They argued with him.	I mentioned their argument with him.

10. They objected to that.	I mentioned their objection to that.
11 They associated with him.	I mentioned their association with him.
12. They intervened in that.	I mentioned their intervention in that.
13. They adjusted to that.	I mentioned their adjustment to that.
14. They quarreled with him.	I mentioned their quarrel with him.
15. They qualified for that.	I mentioned their qualification for that.
16. They believed in that.	I mentioned their belief in that.

Conversation A

S1. Didn't Alice seem anxious about taking the examination?
S2. Yes. She seemed to have a great deal of anxiety about it.
S1. But she's the most intelligent student in the class!
S2. I guess intelligence and anxiety aren't directly related.

Conversation B

S1. Fred seems to be a very sincere and ambitious person.
S2. Yes. I admire his sincerity and ambition a great deal.
S1. I suspect some people are very envious of his success.
S2. Well, I'm sure successful people get quite accustomed to envy.

Conversation C

S1. Did Bill's humorous comments amuse everyone?
S2. Yes, they did. He's very clever, isn't he?
S1. Yes, and he has a good sense of humor.
S2. I think everyone enjoyed his cleverness and humor.

Conversation D

S1. We're very grateful for all your generosity.
S2. You're very kind to express your gratitude.
S1. Well, you were very generous, and we wanted to thank you.
S2. And I have appreciated your kindness.

Conversation E

S1. Did your friends give you an accurate description of the event?
S2. Yes. In fact, their accuracy was very impressive.
S1. They're always very competent and reliable in things like that.
S2. Competence and reliability are important qualities in our work.

Exercise 1

1.	He's very intelligent.	His intelligence is quite apparent.
2.	He's very anxious.	His anxiety is quite apparent.
3.	He's very humorous.	His humor is quite apparent.
4.	He's very clever.	His cleverness is quite apparent.
5.	He's very sincere.	His sincerity is quite apparent.
6.	He's very ambitious.	His ambition is quite apparent.
7.	He's very envious.	His envy is quite apparent.
8.	He's very successful.	His success is quite apparent.
9.	He's very accurate.	His accuracy is quite apparent.
10.	He's very competent.	His competence is quite apparent.
11.	He's very reliable.	His reliability is quite apparent.
12.	He's very grateful.	His gratitude is quite apparent.
13.	He's very generous.	His generosity is quite apparent.
14.	He's very kind.	His kindness is quite apparent.
15.	He's very honest.	His honesty is quite apparent.
16.	He's very diligent.	His diligence is quite apparent.
17.	He's very proud.	His pride is quite apparent.
18.	He's very restless.	His restlessness is quite apparent.

Exercise 2

1.	It was available.	Availability was important.
2.	It was convenient.	Convenience was important.
3.	It was clever.	Cleverness was important.
4.	It was dangerous.	Danger was important.
5.	It was original.	Originality was important.
6.	It was useful.	Usefulness was important.
7.	It was efficient.	Efficiency was important.
8.	It was beautiful.	Beauty was important.
9.	It was stiff.	Stiffness was important.
10.	It was familiar.	Familiarity was important.
11.	It was urgent.	Urgency was important.
12.	It was soft.	Softness was important.
13.	It was dependable.	Dependability was important
14.	It was steady.	Steadiness was important.
15.	It was peculiar.	Peculiarity was important.
16.	It was long.	Length was important.
17.	It was comfortable.	Comfort was important.
18.	it was accurate.	Accuracy was important

Exercise 3

1. He's a wealthy person.   His wealth helps him a lot.
2. He's a strong person.   His strength helps him a lot.
3. He's a neat person.   His neatness helps him a lot
4. He's a wise person.   His wisdom helps him a lot.
5. He's an energetic person.   His energy helps him a lot.
6. He's an intelligent person.   His intelligence helps him a lot.
7. He's a courageous person.   His courage helps him a lot.
8. He's an important person.   His importance helps him a lot.
9. He's a practical person.   His practicality helps him a lot.
10. He's a brilliant person.   His brilliance helps him a lot.
11. He's a lucky person.   His luck helps him a lot.
12. He's an ingenious person.   His ingenuity helps him a lot.
13. He's a mature person.   His maturity helps him a lot.
14. He's an ambitious person.   His ambition helps him a lot.
15. He's an able person.   His ability helps him a lot.
16. He's an independent person.   His independence helps him a lot.

Exercise 4

1. We're aware of her honesty.   She's honest with us.
2. We're aware of your confidence.   You're confident in us.
3. We're aware of his patience.   He's patient with us.
4. We're aware of their fear.   They're afraid of us.
5. We're aware of his antagonism.   He's antagonistic toward us.
6. Were aware of her gratitude.   She's grateful to us.
7. We're aware of your strictness.   You're strict with us.
8. We're aware of their tolerance.   They're tolerant of us.
9. We're aware of her politeness.   She's polite to us.
10. We're aware of his cooperation.   He's cooperative with us.

11. We're aware of their criticism.   They're critical of us.

12. We're aware of her rudeness.   She's rude to us.

13. We're aware of his competition.   He's competitive with us

14. We're aware of their helpfulness.   They're helpful to us.

15. We're aware of her loyalty.   She's loyal to us.

16. We're aware of his neglect.   He's neglectful of us.

Exercise 5

1. She was aware of that.   We noticed her awareness of that.

2. She was absent from that.   We noticed her absence from that.

3. She was ready for that.   We noticed her readiness for that.

4. She was familiar with that.   We noticed her familiarity with that.

5. She was optimistic about that.   We noticed her optimism about that.

6. She was anxious about that.   We noticed her anxiety about that.

7. She was skillful at that.   We noticed her skill at that.

8. She was grateful for that.   We noticed her gratitude for that.

9. She was doubtful about that.   We noticed her doubt about that.

10. She was intolerant of that.   We noticed her intolerance of that.

11. She was proficient in that.   We noticed her proficiency in that.

12. She was sorry about that.   We noticed her sorrow about that.

13. She was responsible for that.   We noticed her responsibility for that.

14. She was successful in that.   We noticed her success in that.

Exercise 6

1. She's dependent on them.
Her dependence on them is obvious.

2. She's considerate of them.
Her consideration of them is obvious.

3. She's intimate with them.
Her intimacy with them is obvious.

4. She's courteous to them.
Her courtesy to them is obvious.

5. She's angry at them.
Her anger at them is obvious.

6. She's suspicious of them.
Her suspicion of them is obvious.

7. She's loyal to them.
Her loyalty to them is obvious.

8. She's jealous of them.
Her jealousy of them is obvious.

9. She's hostile toward them.
Her hostility toward them is obvious.

10. She's cruel to them.
Her cruelty to them is obvious.

11. She's envious of them.
Her envy of them is obvious.

12. She's generous with them.
Her generosity with them is obvious.

Exercise 7

1. They're very ignorant.
People notice their ignorance.

2. She's very proud.
People notice her pride.

3. We're very formal.
People notice our formality.

4. He's very weak.
People notice his weakness.

5. You're very fluent.
People notice your fluency.

6. She's very innocent.
People notice her innocence.

7. I'm very clumsy.
People notice my clumsiness.

8. He's very stupid.
People notice his stupidity.

9. You're very friendly.
People notice your friendliness.

10. She's very popular.
People notice her popularity.

11. I'm very frank.
People notice my frankness.

12. They're very brave.
People notice their bravery.

13. You're very obedient.
People notice your obedience.

14. We're very punctual.
People notice our punctuality.

15. He's very violent.
People notice his violence.

16. She's very appreciative.
People notice her appreciation.

Exercise 8

1.	That'll be simple.	They'll see the simplicity of it.
2.	That was reckless.	They saw the recklessness of it.
3.	That's been precise.	They've seen the precision of it.
4.	That can be consistent.	They can see the consistency of it.
5.	That should be influential.	They should see the influence of it.
6.	That's advantageous.	They see the advantage of it.
7.	That's been probable.	They've seen the probability of it.
8.	That was appropriate.	They saw the appropriateness of it.
9.	That used to be beneficial.	They used to see the benefit of it.
10.	That's suitable.	They see the suitability of it.
11.	That's been possible.	They've seen the possibility of it.
12.	That was foolish.	They saw the foolishness of it.
13.	That ought to be sufficient.	They ought to see the sufficiency of it.
14.	That'll be reliable.	They'll see the reliability of it.
15.	That's been effective.	They've seen the effectiveness of it.
16.	That would be advisable.	They would see the advisability of it.

Conversation Drill A

S1. What did you say about the man?
S2. I said the man ___(A)___ that.
S1. Yes, and his ___(B)___ caused problems.
S2. I guess no one expected that.

(A)	(B)
discovered	discovery
invented	invention
refused	refusal
explained	explanation
criticized	criticism
defended	defense
improved	improvement
discussed	discussion

Conversation Drill B

S1. Do you know Mary very well?
S2. Yes, I do. I know that she's very ___(A)___
S1. Some people aren't aware of her ___(B)___
S2. I've been aware of it for some time.

(A)	(B)
anxious	anxiety
accurate	accuracy
intelligent	intelligence
efficient	efficiency
humorous	humor
clever	cleverness
sincere	sincerity
modest	modesty

Index

The entries below have been selected to aid the student; the index is not all-inclusive. Each entry is followed by the page number and then, in parentheses, the conversation, exercise, or section in which the subject referred to appears. Cross references are also given in parentheses.